WHO IS TH

To benefit from this 2nd edition of my book
prepared to do something new and get out
passionate about sharing your business with the world and, ...
be willing to embrace new opportunities and think positively about change
during your entrepreneurial journey. You could be:

- An entrepreneur;
- Working in sales/marketing;
- Wanting to start a business;
- Someone who has been in business for three years and turning over up to £1 million online;
- In a job and looking for a second income;
- An action-orientated individual;
- A person who is passionate about making a difference.

The practical benefits you'll get from this book are:
- Breaking old habits and building new ones;
- Building blocks for a 21st century business;
- Learning how to use technology to grow your business through sales and marketing;
- Gaining the confidence to share your business online, knowing it will solve your target customers' pain.

This book is NOT for you if:
- You pick things up and never finish them;
- You skim read books and skip to a chapter midway through because you think you know what the first chapter is going to tell you;
- You've spent your time/money working with an agency to build your online presence and it hasn't worked out for you.

If you keep doing what you're doing, you'll keep getting the same results, nothing will change.

To get the results you want, you need to stop and take a fresh approach. Everything I share with you in this book is based on real life examples that I or my clients have personally experienced. To really benefit from what this book has to offer, read from the beginning to the end. It's not going to help you if read Chapter 1 then jump straight to Chapter 6. You need to develop a progressive understanding of why you're doing what you're doing to take away the full power of the messages in this incredibly practical and hands-on guidebook.

WHY A 2ND EDITION?

"RELEVANCE
—— *and* ——
PERSONALISATION"

How your future customers and clients engage with you and your brand has changed, forever.

The digital revolution, through the use of Technology and A.I. (Artificial intelligence), has transformed the way we do business, and there is no turning back.

I've been using social networks since 2004. In the last 10 years everything has changed - and I've seen most of those changes over the last three years.

We need not only to be passionate about our business and laser focused on who our customers/clients are, but also to become media businesses producing relevant content. To be relevant, that content has to be personal, and must connect with our target customer and the different stages of their buying cycle.

This is why I felt the need to update, revise and expand this book to help you be successful online and in growing your business.

WHAT OTHERS SAY

"This book has helped my business grow! I purchased the book at an exhibition and it has helped me develop my business and now I have built my website and my mobiles app, I am able to utilise the power of Social Media through the Click & Shop Facebook page, as well as Twitter and LinkedIn. The book is value for money especially if you are starting out in business and need some guidance, and Warren points you in the right direction."
- Shaun Coleman.

"I have thoroughly enjoyed reading Warren Knight's engaging book, 'Think #Digital First'. Warren's lessons and practical advice in Social Media Optimisation have proved to be invaluable as I help my daughter to set up her new business. It has opened up a whole new world of possibilities. Warren educates, inspires and motivates. I highly recommend this book to anyone wanting to learn about effective digital marketing."
- Naheed Tourish.

"This book is just brilliant for anyone needing to get their head around the world of digital. It's written very clearly and is easy to follow, without being too technical. It covers all the basics you need to know about SEO, social media and all the digital platforms you need - and in a practical step by step manner. I highly recommend it - a really good guide from start to finish!"
- Victoria Peppiatt.

"Making the most of a digital opportunity is about being aware of available tools, a commitment to keeping up to date with what's new and coming online, and an openness to seek advice from digital experts. One of those experts is Warren Knight, and in this helpful book he sets out the key things you need to know to think digital and grow your business. It's a must-read book to help you on your digital way."
- Emma Jones, Founder of Enterprise Nation.

"Marketing is not a standalone and this book takes business owners very effectively through all of the aspects of a company that need to be considered to build a great marketing strategy. Warren reminds us that for marketing to be effective the business must be in good shape first. Far more than just a theory, he provides practical step-by-step actions and tools to implement. It is a great guide for any business owners."
- Joanna Hill, COO Start Up Loans.

"Warren Knight has not only shared his extensive research - and what a resource that is - but his personal experience in this latest book on Digital Marketing. He holds nothing back in his bid to offer help to both the new and growing entrepreneur."
- Guy Clapperton, Author, This Is Social Media.

"I can't say this is the first marketing book I have bought, but it has definitely been the most useful one to date. When you're running your own business, you want and need something punchy, to the point, but which fully explores the subject matter so you can absorb it quickly and effectively. This is one of those books!"
- Joanna Darrell.

"This book is written in distinct Warren style. It is authentic and aims to present the journey of an entrepreneur in easy, manageable steps. It lets you into the life of the writer and challenges you to always learn from your mistakes and successes. Believe me when I say I have read several books aimed at SMEs but this is by far my best read because it tells a story too."
- Justina Ilochi.

"Digital Marketing changes all the time and with the recent internet boom the topic can easily be overwhelming to budding entrepreneurs who need to get their word out there quickly and easily. This book is presented with common sense and simple, practical steps that anyone can pick up and get traction from. Ideal for anyone looking to help their business or other businesses to get seen and heard more easily to drive new sales through digital marketing."
- Daryl Woodhouse.

"One of the only books I've read on Sales and Digital Marketing that provides practical, step-by-step advice, which is really refreshing - as after reading for just a few hours, I walked away with numerous practical tips I could implement in my business right away."
- Pete Campbell.

"I found this book a real delight to read. As an entrepreneur myself, I am always on the lookout for cost-effective strategies to reach new audiences. This book gave me plenty of food for thought, and allowed me to sell more of my own books as well as pick up more clients. This is a must read for any entrepreneur!"
- David Fletcher.

"This book is a must for small businesses and is very easy to read and understand. It is packed full of great, interesting and highly relevant content and I use it as a refresh and reference book. I thoroughly recommend this book whether you are a startup or an established business."
- Carole Black.

"Having known Warren for 20 years I can say he is a true entrepreneur. Warren has definitely found his home in the digital sector. Identifying opportunities and taking on challenges, he is adaptable and sharp minded. Warren has shown that he is adept at integrating and most importantly; creating value for his clients. I highly recommend that you invest in Think #Digital First on your journey to greater success in the digital sphere in your life".
- Karl Pearsall, YesGroup worldwide founder.

MY GIFT TO YOU

The success of your business is not just down to hard work or having a great idea. Part of succeeding is having support and advice from like-minded peers and a thorough understanding of how to use digital marketing tools effectively.

I set up Think Digital First to help ambitious businesses grow and succeed. As well as offering a host of free resources to read, watch, and download (which I share with you throughout the book), I also offer a variety of different courses, all of which are CPD certified.

If, after reading this book you want 'more', I have a very special offer for you, and this is something I have never done before.

As well as holding this '25 years in the making' book in your hand, you will see below a promotional code.

This code will give you a MASSIVE 50% off all of my online courses.

Hundreds of entrepreneurs have joined me and grown their business through the variety of courses that I offer, including, to name a few, my Social Media Boot Camp, 21-Day LinkedIn System, Image Marketing Mastery and Blogging For Success.

If you're ready to take the next step, take advantage of the code below and join me, and hundreds of thriving entrepreneurs, online!

Use code: **TDF50** to receive 50% off

Go here to view the latest online courses: www.thinkdigitalfirst.com/products

Warren Knight
Creator | Think Digital First

ABOUT ME
Award-winning Entrepreneur

I am the creator of Think Digital first, a Top-100 Global Influencer in 2017 and an award-winning blogger, author and digital entrepreneur with 10 years' online experience.

I started my career as a professional hip-hop dancer and am now an international keynote speaker, author and coach, having built a £1m technology company in less than two years.

My vision is, by the end of 2019, to help 100,000 entrepreneurs and business owners successfully sell more products and services online through the strategic use of social media, digital marketing and e-commerce.

DEDICATED TO

What we do today shapes the future.

For me, this has taken on a whole new meaning, all because of one amazing woman who came into my life when I was ready to accept love into my heart.

Zoe, my best friend, my wife and the mother to our beautiful daughter – thank you for opening my eyes and helping me to embrace life in a very different way, which has changed me forever.

I don't know how I can ever compensate for the love you have given me over these past few years. Your affection, understanding, patience and ongoing support, and always being there to listen and be by my side at every step of our journey.

You amaze me. Every day.

This book is dedicated to the two amazing women in my life; my wife, and my daughter Dixie Alberta Knight.

Waking up and falling asleep each day with the infectious smile of our 'little bean' – the little girl who chose us to be her parents after everything we went through – has made the new parent in me want to leave a legacy, and empower change for the better. Change that will live on as she goes from crawling to walking, talking, getting an education and having life experiences to, when ready, embracing the magic of being a parent (I know you feel the same way, Zoe).

You're so tiny, yet your big personality and strength drive me to live longer and be here with you to watch you live life to the full.

Thank you to you both. You have made my life worth living.

I will always love you xx

Published by
Filament Publishing Ltd
16 Croydon Road, Beddington, Croydon,
Surrey, CR0 4PA, United Kingdom.
Telephone +44 (0)20 8688 2598
www.filamentpublishing.com

Disclaimer: This book is for educational and informational purposes only, to suggest choices. It should not be considered medical, legal or financial advice. It is not a replacement for professional diagnosis, medication, or therapy.

ISBN 978-1-912256-28-0

Printed by 4Edge.

DEFINITION OF AN ENTREPRENEUR

Traditionally, an entrepreneur is defined as someone who goes through the process of designing, launching and building a new business, but for me, it is a whole lot more.

An entrepreneur is someone who sees an opportunity that others do not recognise.

"When everything seems to be going against you, remember that the airplane takes off against the wind, not with it."
- Henry Ford

An entrepreneur has an unshakeable self-belief that through hard-work and dedication, an opportunity can turn into a successful business.

An entrepreneur is not discouraged, and is willing to learn, adapt and grow as an individual.

"If you're not a risk taker, you should get the hell out of business."
- Ray Kroc, founder of McDonald's.

An entrepreneur is willing to work hard and personally invest in their journey to success.

"Always deliver more than expected."
- Larry Page, co-founder of Google.

Entrepreneurship may come in many forms, and the desire to make money is just one part of it. All entrepreneurs (me included) set out to change the world, however big or small that change may be.

"The way to get started is to quit talking and begin doing."
- Walt Disney, co-founder of the Walt Disney Company.

CONTENTS

FOREWORD

With more than 1 billion people now online, and increasingly looking for British made products and services, it's become essential for Britain's small businesses to embrace the web and go digital.

The cost to get online is low and yet the benefits run deep. With template website builders, you can have a home on the web for less than £50 and then, leveraging social media, attract people from across the world to visit that website to browse or buy.

Tools such as Twitter, Pinterest, Facebook and LinkedIn have enabled the small business owner to look and think big and to do so on a budget.

What's required to make the most of this digital opportunity is awareness of the available tools, a commitment to keeping up to date with what's new and coming online, and an openness to seek advice from digital experts.

One of those experts is Warren Knight and in this helpful book he sets out the key things you need to know to think digital and grow your business.

Warren starts with advice that 'working on yourself is just as important as building your business' and goes on to offer tips, tools and techniques to understand your customers, engage with them across the web, network with confidence, create actionable plans and how to make the most of your working day!

His knowledge is based on years of experience of supporting entrepreneurs. It's a must read book to help you on your digital way.

Emma Jones – MBE founder of Enterprise Nation

INTRODUCTION

25 YEARS IN THE MAKING

HIP HOP DANCER TO ENTREPRENEUR

HIP-HOP DANCER TO ENTREPRENEUR

From professional hip hop dancer to father; here's my story, 25 years in the making.

It's 1983 and it's a Saturday. Today is the day I get my pocket money. I'm making so much noise in the kitchen, willing my Dad to wake up. I can hear his footsteps leaving the bedroom and approaching the top of the stairs. As he comes down, I run from the kitchen to meet him and, with a smile on his face, he gives me my £1 pocket money. I open the garage door, grab my flame red Raleigh Grifter and cycle to our local village. We live in a little village called Studham, next to Whipsnade Zoo in Bedfordshire, and it takes about 10 minutes to pedal as fast as my little legs can take me. Passing my friends' houses, the local garage, and heading into the village past the Red Lion, (owned by the parents of my first crush Phoebe), I finally make my way to (in my opinion) the world's best sweet shop: Maisy's.

I get off my bike, lean it against the glass window and walk through the door, where a little bell chimes and alerts Maisy's attention. She looks up and says, "Good morning, Warren," to which I reply in a high-pitched voice (as my voice hasn't broken yet), "Morning, Maisy". "Would you like the usual, Warren?" Maisy says, and of course, my usual was none other than cola cubes. She twists the blue lid off, picks up a little yellow scooper and scoops a 1/4 worth of cola cubes into a little white bag. Twisting the bag around and around so it's closed, she hands it to me with a big smile on her face. I give her my £1 from my Dad, get my change and leave the shop.

I get back on my bike and cycle home as fast as I can, hoping one of my friends, Chris, Kevin or Nigel would be outside playing, so I could share with them the journey I'd just been on and offer them a cola cube (if they were lucky).

Fast forward - to being a little bit older, a little bit wiser and with a few extra grey hairs.

I live in Kent, and it's a Sunday. I go down to the cherry farm, around the corner from where I live, and collect my weekly kilo of Sunburst cherries. I walk over to Paul, the owner of the cherry farm and he says, "Morning, Warren, the usual?" I respond in my now broken voice, "Morning, Paul. Yes please, a kilo of Sunburst cherries". He starts weighing the cherries and I ask him to hold on a second. Why? To take a live photo. I pull out my iPhone7, take a picture of the cherries, check-in to my location and share the image across four different social networks to more than 100,000 people, in a split second.

The reason I've shared these stories with you is to highlight how the world has evolved with the use of technology. Even though our natural human instinct has not.

This book will take you through the process of helping you to embrace technology, to Think #Digital First and focus on getting online, and growing a successful business.

Entrepreneurship was in my blood from a young age; making chocolates at night with my mum to make some extra money at school.

In 1986, my passion became a lot more realistic, and looking back now I can see that this is when I started to pave my way to my career as a business owner. I was listening to Capital Radio, with Tim Westwood's usual Hip Hop Show booming from my Bush double tape deck stereo. A year later, the film 'Breakdance' was released, and from that moment I was hooked on learning how to lock, pop, break and do the 'turtle'.

I passed my driving test at 17 and borrowed my Dad's car so I could drive with my friends to London, more specifically to Camden Palace (now Koko's) to bust-a-move. This made me realise my passion for all types of music from Jazz and Hip-Hop to Funk and Soul.

"PROFESSIONAL
hip hop
DANCER,,

Fast forward to 1989, now with fashionably long hair. Illegal raves were sprawled across the national newspapers and TV was talking about the new phenomenon of kids partying in fields 'til sunrise, with DJs spinning tunes all night. I loved to dance and I soon realised I could make a profession out of entertaining people. When I was spotted and asked to dance on stage for a fee, I was delighted and surprised. How amazing to be paid £100s to do what I love, and at that moment I knew I had to make a move and go with this new opportunity. At the age of 20, I moved to London and immersed myself in the music scene. I auditioned for a TV show called Dance Energy, hosted by Normski. A week later, I was on live TV in front of millions of people, doing what I loved; dancing professionally.

In 1991, when the World Wide Web (www) was launched, I spotted a niche in the clubbing scene and used the web to launch the first drum and bass club. I set this up during the day on a Sunday, at The Gardening Club, in Covent Garden. The venue was perfect for giving clubbers the feeling of it still being night time. Soon I expanded, and hired venues including The Old Limelights; and Kensington High Street; mixing house music with drum and bass for special day/night events during Bank Holidays and New Year's Eve. As amazing as it was to be out partying all night and sleeping during the day, I soon realised that I wanted a real business; one where I could wake up on a Monday morning with a coffee, go to my office, dial up to the internet via a modem and start working.

"IN 1991 THE WWW
—— *was* ——
LAUNCHED "

1992, the first birthday of the www, and I wanted to start a business. I needed help from people who knew how to set up and run one. So I approached The Prince's Youth Business Trust. I was offered business training, help preparing my first business plan and, six months later, a loan of £5,000. My first real commercial business, Melodic Distribution, was born. It was a clothing and music (12" record and mix tapes) partnership company which started distributing industry-recognised brands, such as Ministry of Sound, Strictly Rhythm and Dee Jay Recordings. I began doing trade shows in the UK and Europe, selling nationally as well as internationally.

I and my business partner at the time quickly realised that a business cannot survive on 15% commission, so we opened a stall in Camden to sell direct to consumers. This was at a time in the 90s when eCommerce barely existed for small businesses. However, we very quickly understood that what the customer needed and wanted was guiding us as to what to buy.

After a couple of great years, I and my business partner realised that we wanted to go in different directions and embark on our own separate business careers. In 1995, I stepped down as Director and set up my own 'State Of The Art' clothing range selling skateboard/snowboard t-shirts, sweats, hoodies and bags. After sponsoring the UK No.1 skateboarder at the time, my business grew very quickly. I then discovered that my ex-partner had closed down Melodic Distribution, which left a gap in the market. So I decided to partner up with the only company which was recording events up and down the country, converting them into mix tapes and distributing them. This is where Two Tribes (yes, even back in the 90s I was thinking about building tribes) was born.

By the start of 1997, I was burnt out. I had lost focus and started to feel depressed, under pressure, and I closed down Two Tribes. The next few months were difficult. I stayed at home feeling sorry for myself. I didn't exercise or eat. I'll never forget one cold autumn evening when my partner at the time came home and had had enough of my negativity. She walked through the door and said, "I never know what mood you're going to be in when I come home and it makes me nervous every time I put the key in the door and wonder what I'm going to walk into".

That was a major turning point for me; and it made me realise that if I didn't do something about the way I was feeling, no one could do it for me.

The following day I walked into our local shop, brought the paper and started searching for sales jobs because I knew sales was one thing I was good at. Going through the classified ads, I saw a small advert looking for salespeople to cover London and various other local counties. Being from Bedfordshire and going to school in Hertfordshire, I felt qualified to go for an interview. I called the number on the advertisement and was asked to come in that afternoon for an interview. I got the job. Even though it was commission only, I had a purpose again - a reason to get up in the morning and to believe in myself again.

Two weeks into the job, I went into a local London business to discuss how I could help them save money. The meeting went on longer than I had planned, and little did I know that the owner of the business had seen something in me he liked. It was close to lunchtime and he invited me to lunch at a local Italian restaurant, where he asked me how I'd got the job, and lots of questions about my past. Unbeknown to me, he was interviewing me for a sales role in a company that produced goods in China and sold in the UK and Europe.

He offered me the job, and two weeks later I was visiting a trade show in Birmingham called Autumn Fair and meeting the other members of staff with a view to starting work with them a week later. Someone had seen the potential in me, and to this day I have never forgotten that moment. This experience taught me to look past the now, to dig deeper into the past and to think about the future when meeting someone for the first time.

HIP-HOP DANCER TO ENTREPRENEUR

In 2000, I was a Sales Director managing a team of global sales people with a company turning over millions of pounds. During that time, we designed a unique product that was sold to Children In Need and produced for ASDA. The product was spotted by a Disney representative in Hong Kong and, because we had the patent, we were offered a licence to produce all the future Disney characters. In the space of three years, we went from a seven-figure turnover to an eight-figure turnover company. I personally sold into 30 countries from Russia to USA and to South America, utilising the UK Trade and Investment service called OMIS (Overseas Market Introduction Service).

I visited our factory in China three or four times a year and was travelling for a minimum of 10 days a month to see potential clients, and attending trade shows in different countries nearly every month. At one stage, I remember being on a plane, getting a taxi to the hotel and going from the hotel to the Expo and back again. I was in a kind of love/hate relationship with travelling and hotels.

During my time travelling, I bumped into an old friend from my Hip Hop and clubbing days, who was in my industry. He was focused on personal development and invited me to learn more about it. I embraced it with open arms and, before I knew it, I had a new zest for life. I started building my knowledge, learning more and more, meeting some amazing people with amazing stories, and became part of a Mastermind Group. We met up once a month helping each other to become better people, solving problems, and making introductions to move forward in our personal lives or professional careers.

In 2006 my whole life changed in a single phone call. A member of my family was not well and was getting worse. With the rest of my family, I went to the doctors meeting at the hospital with the doctors and the news was even worse than I had expected – in fact, it was incurable. For the last nine years, I had been so consumed with myself and my life that I'd forgotten about the people I loved the most. Yes, looking back, I was being supportive in the only way I thought I knew how. I had my own problems to deal with and was blinkered to what.was happening – right under my nose.

At that moment of realisation, I said to myself, "if I can achieve one million dollars a month in sales I can do anything". So I gave up work for eight months and did everything I could to help turn this horrible situation into something more positive.

During the next eight months, I had to speak in public for the first time. This was in front of 1,000 people about a fundraising campaign to pay for medical costs in the USA. There was a team of us who appeared on national TV, the front pages of national newspapers, TV talk shows and radio talk shows. We were running events from nightclubs, holding celebrity auctions and much, much more. I'd never been on a journey of so many highs and lows. At one very low point, I remember feeling totally broken and it hit me that whatever we were doing was not going to change the outcome. That feeling became a reality, and the life we were fighting for ended very suddenly.

I spent the next few months wondering what all the effort was for, and why we couldn't change what was destined to happen. One significant moment was when I received a phone call from the founder of a charity we'd been working with throughout our campaign. It was a charity fighting to save the life of the Founder's son, although, ultimately, he lost his battle.

At the funeral, the Founder pulled me to one side and said, "two people who came forward during our campaign and donated blood have saved the lives of two other children." I burst into tears. It made me realise that it's not always about the destination, but rather the journey that we go on. Life is full of surprises.

I went back to work for the same firm and, after 12 months of getting over our family's loss, I decided to focus on one magical moment from the campaign. It was when one of the premiership footballers, Jermain Defoe, who we'd been working with very closely, spoke about our campaign on Facebook and promoted our website. During the next 24 hours, we had more hits to the website than we'd ever seen in one day. Offers of help both in time and money came rolling in. I realised that day how powerfully an influencer in a social network, can engage with their audience and get them to take action. Yes, it was an emotional ask, but nevertheless the results spoke for themselves. So I decided I'd had enough of working with Disney and selling into corporates like ASDA, Sainsbury's, New Look, M&S and international retailers. It was time for a change.

By 2008 I really understood the power of the internet and how it can help companies reach their target audience without having to travel around the world, or set up trade shows at an extortionate cost without ever knowing if you will receive a ROI (return on investment).

After researching the best internet marketers globally, I discovered that America was leading the world. At that time, a few UK organisations were inviting these American experts to share their knowledge with small groups of people, for a cost, in the hope of applying their learning to their businesses.

I was fascinated by what I saw going on and decided to write a book about it. In fact, I decided to write four books, as I have never really done things by half. The first book was a sales book about how I achieved $1million sales in one month and the strategy behind that process.

"$1 MILLION SALES
in
ONE MONTH,,

The second book explained how a UK-based business can sell and grow internationally by setting up offices, distributors and partners in various countries. With the experience I'd gathered during my Disney days, I felt I had knowledge to give to others, and I put this first-hand experience into my first business books.

The third and fourth books were about social media for business. I'd spent the best part of a year understanding this new landscape, and I wanted to let people know how they could use it to build their brand, locally, and internationally.

I felt ready to help companies understand social media to achieve brand growth and increase sales. I decided to return to the trade shows that I once disliked so much; this time not as an exhibitor, but as a speaker. I knew that, if I could speak to a room full of people in my industry who were there to listen and learn, I could turn my years of knowledge into a useful journey for them; and a business for me.

I found an amazing designer who developed my first Warren Knight brand and built me a website that reflected my knowledge and showed how I could help companies to grow. I have always done things that I am passionate about, but at this point on my career journey, I felt I had found something I truly loved and was good at, which also added value to other people: public speaking.

However, being good wasn't good enough for me, as, although changing industry and business models wasn't easy, encouraging companies to embrace the power of the internet and digital marketing was a hard task. After several personal setbacks, including getting divorced and giving up work for eight months, I was not in a good financial situation and I started to feel frustrated. I knew I needed help.

The help I needed came in the form of someone who had been very successful in their life, against many odds. I had the utmost respect for him, so I asked him to be my mentor. After he came to watch me speak at an event, we sat in his car for nearly two hours talking. Everything he said about me was true and, although it brought me to tears, I knew he was the right person to help me move to the next stage in my professional and personal life.

For the next three months, I had the most intense emotional rollercoaster of a ride, learning to truly understand myself and what was important to me. I had to do this so that I could define my next journey. Also, I learnt to understand other people better and because of this, I became a better speaker.

During this time, I had the help of two very different coaches. One, an internationally renowned professional speaker whose style is very structured, but personal, which was what I needed for my talks. The other, a comedian and professional speaker. With this professional help, I finally found the real me and learnt how to bring my personality to the stage in a structured way. In fact, I actually found the perfect combination for my personality type.

By 2010, I was speaking at more and more events and trade shows and to hundreds of companies, learning about their business growth problems.

I began to realise there was a massive gap in the eCommerce market for companies wanting to sell online. At this time, there was no self-service, online store builder that was simple and easy to use and offered a big brand experience like ASOS or John Lewis.

I called a friend of mine called who had helped me out with our fundraising campaign in 2007 and together we discussed the issues that UK brands were facing. I had also conducted marketplace research and discovered there was nothing available that matched what I was talking about. Nothing that incorporated the features, functionality and experience of a big brand whilst utilising the power of social media and digital marketing to grow a business online. My friend loved the idea but wasn't in a position to help me financially. He was a shareholder of a small creative digital agency and suggested I speak to the founders, which I did.

A few weeks later, we'd come up with a new brand, a business model and a route to market. During the next few months his team of developers built the UK's 1st social sharing eCommerce platform, designed to give SMEs a big brand experience offering a multi-channel experience, and Gloople was launched.

In 2011, Gloople (the name came from 'glueing people together') launched and grew very quickly. We started building eCommerce websites for more brands and were winning various awards and many accolades in the industry.

By early 2012, we knew the only way to take the company to the next stage was to attract investment. I engaged with an expert in the industry to help us write a business plan and we prepared a three-year cash flow forecast. Three months later, we were ready to go to market. I presented our proposition to a room full of investors and before I had even finished my presentation an investor walked up to me with his business card and said, "I want to be your lead investor".

Six weeks later, on the 27th September 2012, the funds were in our bank account, valuing the business at just under £1 million in less than two years. To help the investors protect their investment, we were approved for the Seed Enterprise Investment Scheme (SEIS).

We now had the funds to grow the team and build a SaaS (software as a service) platform enabling brands to build their own online store. Two months later, my technology business partner, Julian, became very ill and unable to help the team build a product to revolutionise the online web store space. This caused many concerns for the current shareholders and our investors, so I went back out to the market to find the next round of investment. I also turned to an old friend, Tarquin, whom I'd known for more than 20 years, to either help and/or get involved. I needed to stay focused on sales and continue running a technology team while working with the board members and shareholders. I also needed to prepare a new business plan, with a four-year cash flow forecast and a seven-figure investment.

2013 was about to become one of the most challenging business years I'd ever experienced, and after months and months of preparation, finding investors and approaching new challenges head on, we had run out of cash. In September 2013, we had to liquidate the company. You can imagine how I felt when, after three and half years, I had to walk away from our Shoreditch office and start all over again.

I quickly realised that for every positive and negative thing that had happened to me professionally during the past 25 years, the one thing that I had always learnt was to grow from every situation and stay true to myself.

After Gloople was liquidated, I hit another low in my life. I had lost personal investment, as well as steady income. I had lost everything. I was living on a mattress at a friend's grandparents' flat in Edgware, North London, and found myself spending New Year's Eve on my own because of not wanting to be around anyone.

I woke up on New Year's day 2014 and realised that I am the person 100% in control of my personal and professional goals/career, and started to get excited about the next journey I was about to go into - without even realising what that looked like.

A few days later, I had a conversation with a friend of mine who told me about a Government initiative at that time. This friend made me realise that 20+ years of being in business, as well as my eight years' experience in Social Media and Digital Marketing was a great asset of mine. Start-up companies and business owners would really value my experience, and he suggested that the Government initiative would be the perfect platform to take my knowledge and share it with business owners.

Within the space of 12 months, I had built my coaching business into a six-figure income and managed to turn my life around. During these 12 months, my online presence had grown, and I became a well-known Social Media and Digital Marketing speaker across the UK at various events and tradeshows.

After sharing my knowledge and experience with business owners on a one-to-one basis I began to see that this experience would make a great book. After three months of writing, it was ready to go to print, followed shortly by a book launch in Central London.

The launch date for the first edition of Think #Digital First was in March 2015, where we had a successful day not only selling books, but also live-streaming the event and achieving sales via Amazon. At the book launch I invited somebody who I'd been seeing for a few weeks to come down and meet my friends and family.

In May, I was at The Business Show, as a keynote speaker with 25,000 people intent on starting, or growing a business. My phone rang, and I took the call. The person on the other end told me that the Government initiative (my big source of income) was ending, with immediate effect.

Having won multiple awards for writing, coaching and being an entrepreneur and with a new found passion for being an educator through training, I had seen companies like LinkedIn acquiring Lynda, the largest online training platform. I knew that this left a gap in the market to help start-ups, SME's and corporate employees learn how to use Social Media and Digital Marketing to build brand awareness, generate leads and get sales. That Government initiative phone call made me realise that I needed multiple income streams to ensure that I'd never be in the same position that I was in after having to liquidate Gloople.

One day, after swiping right on Tinder, I fell in love. We both realised that we wanted something out of life that neither of us had ever had, and that was to have a baby.

Because we were both over the age of 40 we decided to not waste any time, and to start on our IVF journey. During this time, I also began to truly understand the psychology of online users by learning from experts who had built multi-million pound business by sharing their knowledge through training people online.

I'll never forget it. Two days before we were about to go on holiday to Ibiza, and our first IVF appointment came through. We were both so excited about the thought of having our first child. During our first meeting, a bombshell was dropped. No more alcohol for me, if I was serious about being a dad. We went away and I drank San Miguel 0.0% (no alcohol beer) all holiday.

We started our first round in August. After hundreds of injections, and dozens of trips to the clinic, we received the bad news; we weren't pregnant.

We decided that this was not the end of our quest to have a child, and opted for a second round, taking on board everything we had learned from the first time round, and committing to a second round at the same clinic. This journey started in October.

By October 2015, I'd managed to take the last eight years of delivering training and build it into an online training program. I decided to do a minimum viable product (MVP) and test to see if people were actually interest in learning what I had to offer. I launched my very first online course, which was a live 6-week Social Media boot camp and in just four weeks of marketing, I had generated more than five figures in profit, which equalled 12 hours of my time delivering the course.

In November we got some amazing news. We were pregnant. After many hours of happy tears, we had finally got what we wanted. I was on cloud nine. Everything was going great in my new business, and in my family life. I had finally got what I wanted.

Unbeknown to the new love of my life, I had spoken to her dad, and asked him the one question that would cement our life together. I asked him for his daughter's hand in marriage. I then went engagement ring shopping with my sister (once I had been given a BIG yes by her dad) and found the perfect diamond ring which I knew she would love. I had planned for Christmas morning to be the morning I would ask the love of my life to be my wife.

On Christmas Eve, we realised something wasn't right. Reality kicked in and my wife-to-be had miscarried. This was the most difficult moment we had faced together as a couple, and we spent all night thinking about our next steps.

On Christmas Day morning, it was time for me to get down on one knee. She said "yes", and we agreed to get married in July the following year. To help plan the next step of our future we decided to go away for New Year. There was nothing better than sun, sea and sand to help us reflect on the past, and plan for our future together.

After two rounds of IVF at the same clinic, we wanted to know 'why' we fell pregnant, and more importantly; why we miscarried. The data driven marketer in me knew it was time to do my research. We decided on a third and final round of IVF at a different clinic.

It took months of testing at the new clinic, and finally in May, we understood the reasons 'why' the miscarriage happened. Now that we understood this, we were ready for our third and final round of IVF. Excitement kicked in again, but there was no hiding how emotionally exhausted we both were.

During this time we decided to leave London after 25 years and move to Kent, as we could visualise a different future as a family outside of London.

The months that followed during our third round of IVF were the most gruelling of my life. We were travelling to London, with two important appointments and injections 3-4 times every single day.

In June we visited the clinic to give a sample of blood to see if we were pregnant. We decided to go to a little café in North London for some lunch and wait for the phone call. The phone rang. It was the clinic. Neither of us wanted to answer the phone (out of fear) so we put it on loudspeaker and waited to hear the results...

POSITIVE. We both cried and the owner came over asking if we were OK, so we told her what had just happened and that we were crying with happiness, and of course she congratulated us. All the hard work and visualising our future as a family had worked. Over the next few months the travelling and injections continued and finally we saw a tiny heartbeat in our seven week scan (I still have the video).

Fast forward to a beautiful summer's day in July. Our friends and family were all dressed in blue (our theme), ready and excited to watch us get married. The church looked stunning and I got married to love of my life. What made this day even more special was that we got married with her being 10 weeks pregnant. It was the best day of my life.

During all of this, I had taken the MVP and the success of the first online course and turned it into a business. I started to go through the process of positioning and branding the new business. I designed the wireframes to build a website with a vision of helping 100,000 entrepreneurs by 2019 through my online education company offering online courses in social media, digital marketing and business growth.

Realising that my time was best spent on growing the business, I knew something had to change. Having worked with my sister Starr for many years (and putting her wrong age in the first edition...sorry Sis) and Jenny my VA in the Philippines, I knew I needed to expand the team.

Now, with four revenue streams and a new hire, focusing specifically on booking events and managing partnerships, I decided to expand the value proposition of the book Think #Digital First by building my first online course and then turning it into an online education company.

Thinkdigitalfirst.com launched in November 2016 offering a range of Social Media and Digital Marketing courses. The launch was a great success, and at this point I had six very successful courses with hundreds of my audience giving me their time to help them grow their business through Digital Marketing.

At the start of 2017 Think Digital First was on target to generate more than six figures, and everything was going great, professionally and personally. My wife; Zoe, and I were eight months pregnant with the imminent arrival of our baby.

And on the 18th February at 5:18am my life changed forever. I became a dad to a beautiful baby girl; Dixie Alberta Knight, born 5 pounds and 10 ounces after an amazing, natural birth. My family was complete.

The newest member of my team was focusing on speaker engagements and building partnerships. The business was thriving. With things from an online perspective changing so much over the last three years, it seemed like the perfect time to rewrite and expand the book; Think #Digital First, which was first written in 2014.

With over 30 speaking engagements booked, 50 webinars and 500 people coming through Think Digital First's online courses, the next three years look to be both exciting and challenging, from a personal and business perspective.

ONE

BEING THE MOST SUCCESSFUL YOU

CHAPTER 1

I found my love for Social Media whilst trying to save the life of a terminally ill family member.

In order to become an expert in your field and have a successful business, you need to have a true passion and love for it; because it's what you're selling.

As I've matured, my priorities have shifted. In my 20s I was passionate about life, and work; making mistakes along the way. In my 30s I tried to settle down, keeping my work and home life very separate. Now I'm in my 40s. I have the same passion for my work, but am married, with a beautiful baby girl, and merging work and family to give me the lifestyle I want.

"IT TAKES 10,000 HOURS *to be an* EXPERT "

I've spent tens of thousands of hours learning, growing and educating myself because success is rarely an overnight thing. Without spending your time, effort and money working on YOURSELF, you will not achieve your goals, realise your vision or create your legacy.

People may look at my online presence without knowing my story and believe that becoming a digital entrepreneur and influencer came easy, when in fact; this couldn't be further from the truth.

I have had some great wins in my life, but I've also had a large number of losses, including a business or two.

If you're thinking about starting a business, take a second, and look at yourself. If you don't have the passion, and WANT to learn and be educated, the road to success will be very long, and impossible.

What do you think is needed to become a successful entrepreneur and thought leader in your industry? Having been there, and done that; I understand what failure looks like when passion for a business idea is not there. I can also say from experience that learning how to love what you do does give you a great starting point to becoming a success.

WHAT MAKES A SUCCESSFUL ENTREPRENEUR?

Becoming a successful entrepreneur is down to truly believing in yourself, and having a good understanding of how to approach the world of business. Here are 10 traits for you to go through, and think about how they apply to you, and why they're important to your success.

Take Time Out For Yourself

I know how difficult it can be to get caught up in the day-to-day workings of life. Just because you might be doing something that you love, doesn't mean you'll love it all the time. I always make sure I have a clear vision for what I want to achieve, and set goals. This not only holds me accountable for what I need to achieve, but also helps me take one step at a time.

Think about how what you do on a day-to-day basis triggers any kind of stress and anxiety, and how you can take time out for yourself to really relax and recharge, so that your business can thrive and you are as productive as possible.

Get Obsessed

We're not talking about being a love-struck teenager. We're talking about what drives you to get out of bed in the morning, and what puts a smile on your face when talking to your friends and family.

Remember that if you don't ENJOY what you do, your happiness will suffer. If you do enjoy what you do it will feel like you never work a day in your life.

I found that changing careers led to me studying more than ever before. I not only had to learn an entirely new world, I also had to become obsessed with it. I wanted to understand the online landscape and what I needed to achieve to get to where I wanted to be.

I now have a growing business, with a strong team, as well as a wife and little girl, and because of my passion, experience and wanting to be a dad who is always around, I have designed my ideal lifestyle and now have a business I run from my office (at home).

What does 'getting obsessed' look like to you? Are you genuinely happy with how your life is going, and if not, how do you get to where you want to go? Self-belief is a strong push for any entrepreneur. Once you believe in what you can achieve, you can face any situation head on and build your future exactly the way you want it to be.

With the 1st edition of this book, I started the process 12 months before its launch, but all the energy I had to give to the project was wrong. So I took a step back, put it down and picked it up again when I was running on full steam.

The 2nd edition (the one you are currently reading) was an: "I need to tell the world about the last three years, and the only way to do it is to write a 2nd edition". We started the journey in April and had finished the final draft by end of May to send to the editor. It then reached the designers and printers by June, ready for the launch in July.

Mapping out a process and a timeline for yourself is a fantastic way to help you know if you have the time and commitment to complete the task. Also, having a dedicated timeline keeps you accountable throughout this process.

Persevere Through Adversity

There are always going to be difficult or uncomfortable situations in business. Perseverance is one of the most valuable tools an entrepreneur can possess.

I spent 12 months building a new ecommerce platform and then taking it to market. A year later, we'd invoiced more than six figures and I was going out for my seed funding. Three months later I received £150,000 investment, valuing my business at £1million in less than two years. Just 12 months later, I had to call the liquidators in, and tell my staff, investors and shareholders I was closing the business.

Some of the greatest lessons and life experiences come from being in an uncomfortable situation, when you have to learn from persevering through adversity.

Writing the original Think #Digital First in 2014 was one of the most difficult experiences of my life, and I learnt a great deal from it. I knew that re-writing this book was going to be difficult, too, but because I'd done it once, although there were always going to be bumps in the road, I was prepared.

I remember the day that I and my soon-to-be wife sat down and discussed going through the IVF process in the hopes of bringing a child into this world. We went through some of the toughest moments in both of our lives, but at the end of our journey, a miracle happened.

If something was smooth sailing, it wouldn't make the successes in the end as great as they are, right?

Invest In Yourself

Throughout my life I have found people with specialist subjects in which I lack knowledge. One of the most important things you need to remember as a business owner is to take everything you learn, and apply it to your business. Investment doesn't just mean money; its means time, too.

I have travelled the world, built relationships with international brands, and invested my time and energy into becoming a better ME. Whilst you may not see this from the outside looking in, I always follow those in my industry who inspire me, by reading their content, attending their webinars and paying (with my hard-earned cash) for their courses.

Part of becoming a success is learning from other people's successes. I was lucky enough to start my journey to becoming a Social Media expert 10 years ago, and this was not only the perfect time for me, but the perfect time for the online world.

The reason I say this is to get you thinking about the NOW. Don't wait another five years before taking the leap into doing something you love, because time is precious, and looking back on life with regrets is how you forget to move forward and achieve your ultimate goal of success online.

Become An Expert

The first time I really found myself researching Social Media was because of a captivating interest in the online world. Whilst my interest first grew from desperation, it became something completely different, and I am now a thought leader in that world.

Finding your customers' pain, and solving it, is what leads to a successful business. Don't just give your audience what THEY want; think ahead. How can you solve their current pain, then pre-empt the next pain and already have it solved?

The end goal for your business from a financial perspective is to have profitable customers. To achieve that end goal, and be seen as an expert in your industry, you need to focus on getting brand awareness. It takes an average eight times for a potential customer to 'touch' your business before they feel ready to buy.

I have members of my audience who have been following everything I do for close to two years, and only NOW are they ready to spend their money with me. And that's OK, because I know that trust has been built and they will become repeat customers.

Be A Planoholic
Realign yourself. Look ahead. Where are you going in the next chapter of your life? It wasn't until I sat in that car with my mentor that I really stopped to question myself.

More recently, when going through my business growth phase and building two websites (both of which talk to a different target audience), I realised that I had to personalise each user journey. I understood this and reached out to my mastermind community, finding two people who helped me understand where I was going wrong and what to do to fix it.

It was a positive experience and gave me the refocus I needed, to see what was important to me. To coin the phrase 'intelligence high, emotions low', I had to commit and make intelligent decisions. Understanding this, and planning my next step, was so important to me, and the growth of my business.

"TWO EARS FOR LISTENING *— and —* ONE MOUTH FOR SPEAKING "

Be Open To Change

You could be reading this book because of the overwhelming feeling of not knowing which way to turn. Have you asked yourself, "why do these things keep happening to me?" I know I have.

There is such a thing as a vicious circle and it's difficult to find a way out of the loop of negative actions once you're bound up in them. There are habits in life that we keep repeating; even knowing they are not good for our personality. Take 'baby steps' when changing the direction of your life, and embrace the changes. Understand that although the way you market online, and the direction your life will take, might change, your values still need to stay the same.

When looking at the changes that are happening, and actually being open to them, think about how you connect with people around you. I'm sure you've heard the saying that we have two of these (ears) and one of those (mouth). In other words, spend more time listening.

To give you an example; the one thing that has stayed constant during the last 25 years is me, and I have never stopped learning or growing. When I was only 20 years old, I experienced the power of this. On stage at a big event, dancing in front of a huge crowd for Shades of Rhythm, I remember misjudging the stage and falling straight into the crowd. I can assure you this never happened again. While I've made many mistakes (some big, some small), I've always learnt from them to become a better person, both in my personal life and in business.

At each stage of your journey, you must always be making notes and evaluating the process, ultimately paying attention to every action, and reaction and systemising. If you're not ready to break the old habits and build new ones, then pause and take some time away from the immediate issue and come back to it later.

Manage Your Money Wisely

How many times have you looked at your bank account and felt worried because you didn't have the cash flow to help you survive, or general income that would cover your monthly costs?

Think about how you can structure your finances, and manage your income and outgoings so that you don't find yourself in a difficult position. I remember living on my friend's grandparents' floor and feeling hopeless, knowing that my income wouldn't allow me to rent a flat and live. So I had no choice but to stay where I was. Looking back on this now, the turning point was when I decided to make the change, manage my money wisely and slowly get myself out of the dark hole that I'd found myself in because of a lack of structure.

An entrepreneur will inevitably have highs and lows when it comes to money, but the best advice I can give you is to always stay on top of your finances, and have a structure in place so that you can prepare should something go wrong.

Stay Up-To-Date With Technology

Audience members who take part in my courses always ask questions about the world of technology being so overwhelming because of the abundance of tools available. Whilst I use a large selection of tools, I know that the world is constantly changing.

As I'm writing this, I've had to remove a specific tool from this book which I used to use on a regular basis, because of the way this piece of technology has changed. Whilst it's still the same tool, it has been acquired by a larger company and, right now, we don't know how it'll be used in the future.

I've also realised that a handful of the tools I spoke about in the first edition have changed their value proposition, closed down as a business or, in most cases, been outranked by a competitor.

Close to 40% of the tools that I've used over the years are no longer available – but it's not about the tool/company you use, it's about the outcome you achieve through using technology. Stay as up-to-date as possible with technology, so that you're always one step ahead of your competitors.

Understand Your Strengths And Weaknesses

Have you ever been in a relationship where, after a few years, you both start to grow in different directions? One way of dealing with this is to write down together the areas where each person feels the other person has changed. You can do the same for yourself.

When you want to get the best results out of what you're doing, you need to focus on the things you like and the things you know you're good at. This gives your mind the power to compare and contrast all your options. Knowing and using what you're good at is empowering. Using strategies that have worked for you before is taking positive action to achieve what you want.

"WHAT DOES YOUR FUTURE LOOK LIKE
— *and* —
HOW ARE YOU GOING TO
GET THERE"

HOW DOING WHAT I LOVE HAS IMPACTED MY LIFE AND HOW IT CAN IMPACT YOURS

Now that I've shared with you the traits of a successful entrepreneur, I would like you to work with me, and write down the answers to the following questions.

Are You Fulfilled?

Warren Knight: Because I am able to manage my businesses from my own home, I can enjoy the best of both worlds; being an entrepreneur and a father. I see a job as being a personal fulfilment, and not just about getting paid.

You:

_____

_____

_____

Are You More Productive?

Warren Knight: Studies show that people who are excited and passionate about their work have a higher productivity rate. Whilst I may be slightly sleep deprived due to now being a father, my productivity is still as strong as ever. My time management and energy management has shifted. My day now starts at 6am so my peak energy levels are in the morning, and will dip early afternoon. Loving what I do helps me meet my challenges face on, and productively work through them.

You:

_____

_____

_____

Are You More Motivated?

Warren Knight: I meet my goals, and when I do; I see how successful I can be. This keeps me motivated and gives me meaning. When I see how happy my customers are with the work I create, it motivates me to keep going.

You:

_____

_____

_____

Are You Motivating Others?

Warren Knight: I genuinely love my job, and my passion shines through whenever I run a live stream, create a video, run a new course or meet a customer in real life. If you let your passion for your work radiate, you motivate others. Being a source of motivation for others has not only impacted my life, but it impacts the work they do to improve themselves. It's important to be motivated by being better than your competitors.

You:

_____

_____

_____

Are You Respected By Family And Peers?

Warren Knight: It is so important to become a role model – someone for people to look up to. Whilst I do have to travel and take time away from my family, my wife always understands, and respects my decisions because she knows I wouldn't do it if it wasn't a meaningful career move.

You:

_____

_____

_____

Has Your Mental Health Improved?

Warren Knight: I went through a lot of dark times in my life that now seem so distant. Having a meaning, and a purpose with the work I do has given me a great mindset to continue on the journey of doing what I love for a living.

You:

_____

_____

_____

Are You Always Looking To Learn?

Warren Knight: Passion leads to the need to keep on learning. Just because people might look at me and see the successes of being an award-winning entrepreneur, doesn't mean that my work stops here.

You:

_____

_____

_____

Are You A Thought Leader?

Warren Knight: I would have never become a thought leader in my industry if my true passion and love for what I do didn't shine through in the work I deliver. With conviction, I have built a large following online that engages with me, and trusts the tweets I share and the blogs I write.

You:

_____

_____

_____

Do You Get Excited About New Challenges?

Warren Knight: Do I get excited about new challenges? Hell yes. I get out of bed every morning, kiss my little girl, and walk into my office to face new challenges, and it puts a smile on my face.

You:

_____

_____

_____

Is Your Work A Chore?

Warren Knight: Truly enjoying what you do gives you the freedom to treat everything you do as though it's a passion, and not just work. This is how you give the best possible YOU to your audience.

You:

_____

_____

_____

Has My Ability To Help Others Improved?

Warren Knight; Whether it's reading an article I have written, listening to one of my live webinars, hearing me speak at an event or working with me through one of my online courses; I always aim to help others. Loving what I do helps others improve which in turn allows me to keep growing as an entrepreneur.

You:

_____

_____

_____

Do You Push Yourself To Succeed?

Warren Knight: I remember watching Matthew McConaughey's Oscar-winning speech for Dallas Buyers Club in 2014 and he said something very important.

"I always need someone to chase. When I was 15 years old, someone important came to me in my life and asked me who was my hero. I thought about it. I know who it is. It's me in 10 years."

Like Matthew McConaughey said, _"every week, every day, every month and every year of my life, my hero is always 10 years away. It gives me someone to keep on chasing"._ Think about that for a minute. Pushing myself to succeed is me looking at what I want to achieve in 10 years, and always having something to aim for.

You:

_____

_____

_____

Doing what you love for a living doesn't come easy. A simple and effective acronym I love to share is K.I.S.S. Keep It Super Simple. This helps me stay laser focused on what's important.

Re-writing this chapter for the second edition showed me how much I have achieved, and how my life has become something I can be proud of, and thank myself for every day.

"KISS

KEEP IT SUPER SIMPLE "

TWO

YOUR FRAMEWORK FOR SUCCESS

CHAPTER 2

What is the end goal for your business? Where do you and your business want to be in three years? Perhaps more importantly right now; where do you see your role in your business in the next 12 months?

I asked myself that exact question when I wrote the first edition of this book, and everything I visualised and put on my vision board has come true, and actually turned out better than I could have imagined. (The only thing I've let slide is the gym, but with a less than 6-month old baby, I'll be gentle on myself.)

- ☑ **Married**
- ☑ **Healthy baby**
- ☑ **Living in the countryside**
- ☑ **Growing the business**
- ☑ **Building the team**
- ☑ **Speaking and training internationally**

To create a framework for success you will need to include the key areas around your business. You must know what these are, so you can build the structure of your business on strong foundations.

Sending a random tweet or uploading a photo to Instagram once a month is not enough Social Media activity for a successful business. For every action (or no action) there is a reaction. You must always ask yourself: what is the outcome I am seeking to get the result I am looking for?

"SOCIAL MEDIA *will not fix a* **BROKEN BUSINESS "**

With thousands of new businesses launching every single month, the future of business growth is through marketing online. All of our future customers will be online, and as businesses we need to change our mindsets and understand how to acquire these clients through Social Media and Digital Marketing.

Consider new trends such as content marketing, marketing automation and artificial intelligence to connect with your potential customers. Once you have your customers' attention, you can use an autoresponder to give them something more, such as your latest catalogue or a report that shows the current industry news. You can do this as a digital download, to make it easier for them. Their name and email automatically go into your email marketing campaign system and you can continue to deliver your marketing message to them; adding value, educating and ultimately getting them to buy what you're selling via your online marketing.

This digital process to acquire new customers sounds amazing, doesn't it?

However, as it is almost impossible to include every aspect of becoming a socially-savvy business, this book breaks it down for you into meaningful grabs. You now have the right mindset to move forward through it, and this chapter looks at the framework necessary to grow a successful business.

Here is my eight-step formula to help you get focused and design a more detailed business plan with a three-year cash-flow.

1. Executive Summary
2. Business Products/Services
3. Target Market and Competition
4. Sales and Marketing
5. Management and Personnel
6. Operation and Assets
7. Finances
8. SWOT Analysis

The first step (even if you've been in business for some years) is to design a simple mini business plan. Trust me, it's not as scary as it sounds and it doesn't have to be as complicated as you expect.

Aligning your business is an intelligent thing to do, so you truly understand where and how your business is going to grow. It doesn't make any difference whether you are a start-up or have been trading for three years. Writing a business plan helps you clarify where you are now and where you want to take your company.

To help you build your business plan, let's elaborate on these points. This will define the next step you take for intelligent growth.

1. EXECUTIVE SUMMARY

An executive summary gives you an overview of what the business is about, covering everything from your team, business model, marketing plan, revenue and target customer. This is also where you would include your 'vision' for your business.

Here are two executive summary examples.

"To provide our customers with safe, good value, point-to-point air services. To effect and to offer a consistent and reliable product and fares appealing to leisure and business markets on a range of European routes. To achieve this we will develop our people and establish lasting relationships with our suppliers." EasyJet

"To organise the world's information and make it universally accessible and useful." Google

Vision Statement Defined

A Vision Statement is a prediction of where your business will be in the future. This can be an emotional driver for those in the company and can be a powerful and purposeful driving force to success. Here are two examples.

"Bringing to the world a portfolio of beverage brands that anticipate and satisfy people, desires and needs." Coca-Cola

"A personal computer in every home, running Microsoft software." Microsoft

2. BUSINESS PRODUCT / SERVICE

Knowing what you're selling, and how you're selling it, to your customers is a crucial step to building a successful operation. As an educator, I've come across many small business owners with the same frustration around using Social Media. What I learnt was that, as most small business owners are time short, they want to improve their knowledge from the comfort of their own home. This was the customer problem that I identified and set out to solve when I founded Thinkdigitalfirst.com.

If you know the pain you're trying to solve, you can find the solution. Both the customer problem and the solution need to be congruent with your business goals.

What is your unique selling proposition? When I was defining the USP for my eCommerce platform, I had to create an elevator pitch, which you can see below.

"The UK's first social sharing eCommerce platform designed for SME's to have a big brand experience".

Let's break this down, so it's clear.
- The target market at that time and for the 12 months was the UK;
- The unique functionality of the platform was the social sharing aspect, and it was the first eCommerce platform to have a Social Media selling feature, which allowed me to use the word first;
- It was an eCommerce platform (does what it says on the tin);
- The target market were SMEs (small to medium sized enterprises); and lastly
- Focus on the benefit, which for us was the ability to give the customer the same experience they would have on a big brand website, such as BooHoo and Asos.

More recently, for my online video training business;

"I want to help 100,000 entrepreneurs sell more products and services through the strategic use of my Social Media and Digital Marketing online video courses."

This is what made us different to our competitors, and you need to spend time figuring out what makes your business unique. Defining your USP takes time; I suggest a night in with your friends, pizzas and beers to help challenge you to get the focused and creative answers you need.

To really understand your USP and whether your business has the potential to be successful in the market, you need to do your due diligence. This will include everything from competitor, industry sector and target market research to solving your customers' pain point. Research is an integral theme throughout this book, demonstrating how completely necessary it is to build strong foundations for a successful, socially-savvy business.

Once your USP has been defined, you can look at your business and decide how you're going to share this with your audience. One question I always ask my clients is, "If you got into a lift with Richard Branson and you only had 30 seconds to describe your business to him, what would your elevator pitch be? Memorising your elevator pitch so you are saying it in your sleep will always guarantee that, at the most opportune moments, you can share what your business does with certainty and clarity.

3. TARGET MARKET AND COMPETITION

A target market is a group of customers towards which a business has decided to aim its marketing efforts, and ultimately its product or service. A well-defined target market is the first component of a marketing strategy and is a critical element of your business strategy. Then you know that your time, energy and money are being spent in the right direction.

> **"NOT EVERYONE** *is your* **TARGET CUSTOMER"**

Deciding on your target market may not be as easy as it seems. It will be time consuming and will take more than just your own input. Firstly, you need to create what I like to call a Wish List.

A Wish List is as simple as specifically defining who is going to buy your product or service. You need to identify your target customer by location, interest, age, gender, income, occupation and marital status. You must recognise that you can't do business with everyone, and creating your own niche target market will allow you to develop your business in the best possible way.

Valuing each different type of customer and making sure your message reflects this is key to your successful sales and marketing. This is the Value Proposition you are giving to your different types of customer and in Chapter 6 I'll be explaining what I mean in more detail.

Being laser-focused on your target market is crucial for your business. Once you define who is going to buy your product or service, you know who is most likely going to need your business and the problem you want to solve. Being a big fish in a small pond rather than vice-versa is a more effective strategy for any small business. It is easier to build your reputation and sales if you are more targeted in your marketing.

Deciding on my target market was not as simple as picking a name and characteristics. You need to look at your own experience, the opportunities around you and your business focus. Think about what you've achieved in the past and the industries you have worked in. In the era of the 'experience,' you have to give your customers an experience they'll fall in love with. For example, Uber and Airbnb have grown to be successful companies because they provide a great customer experience while fulfilling a need.

Put yourself in your target customers' shoes. What is their first thought when researching a product? How do they progress from there? Most importantly, what's the final question they ask before making a purchase?

I now have four revenue streams and two of those have the same target customer, however the other two are completely different.

Someone who buys my book and is interested in one of my online courses is not the same person who will book me to speak at an international conference. I will also work with amazing UK-based businesses with a large database of my target customers over a 12-month roll-out program.

To better understand this exercise, let's analyse two hypothetical target customers: Rita and Sue (it's a boy named Sue).

Rita is more right brain, making her a creative entrepreneur and visual in her approach to business and lifestyle. She's passionate and inquisitive, always asking questions before making a decision to buy a product or service. She calls her friends on the phone, and searches with Google and through Social Media. Rita's way of finding answers is through a Pinterest infographic or an Instagram post.

Here's how you might identify Rita's thought process when purchasing a product or service.

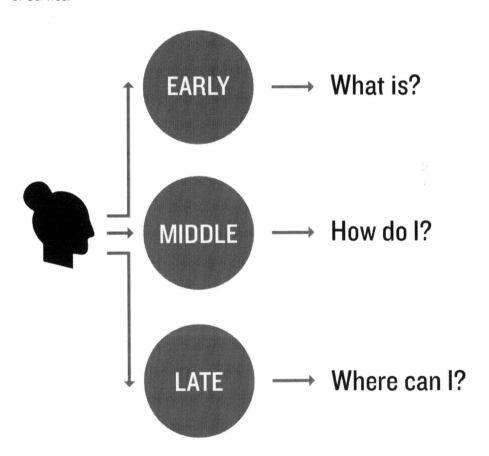

Sue (a boy named Sue) is more left brain, and thinks logically and works on a structured basis through a process-driven environment. He's more interested in facts and figures than Rita, but like Rita, he talks to his friends and uses Google to gather information. He prefers LinkedIn's more B2B approach to getting answers to his questions.

Here's how you might identify Sue's approach to purchasing a product or service.

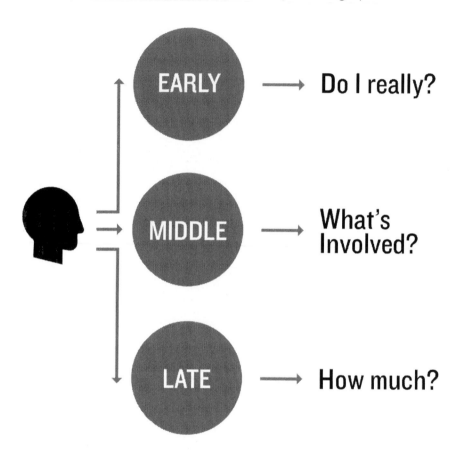

The three stages in the customer acquisition journey are always the same but with a different human approach. Your ideal customers are asking different questions, and your business can build trust by answering their questions and providing valuable content in the form of blog posts, images, infographics, and webinars.

By taking the time to understand how your target customer thinks, you'll better understand what content will resonate with them and how you can earn their trust.

I named my target customers to create a visual in my mind of who I want to buy my product, and once I knew this, my marketing strategy became easier to design. With an image in your mind and characteristics written down, you can avoid the common mistake of thinking that 'everyone is my target customer'.

Ask yourself this question: What is a visitor looking for when they think about my business? Let's simplify this into three segments.

1. **Early (visitor):** This person does not necessarily know that they want your product/service. They are just researching and looking for information to help them make a decision.

2. **Middle (prospect):** They now know that they need what you offer, but they don't yet trust you enough to pay for your product/service. They are looking for help from you to make a decision through the content they download, through testimonials or from an industry influencer who talks about your business.

3. **Late (customer):** They now know, like and trust you, are ready to become a customer, and need to be shown how to work with you.

Your business must speak to this person at each stage of their journey with the same tone of voice.

Now fill out your ideal target customer, and what you think they look like.

GET TO KNOW YOUR PERFECT TARGET CUSTOMER

I live in _____

My name is _____

I drive a _____

I am ____ years old

I earn _____

My skills are _____
_____
_____

I am a _____ (job title)

I read the _____

I watch _____

I love to go to _____

I bank with _____

I like to eat at _____

My favourite sport is _____

I work for _____

The phone I use is _____

I listen to _____

My company turnover is _____

I like to spend my money on _____

My favourite website is _____

My favourite social network is _____

4. SALES AND MARKETING

Throughout this book I'll be touching on various different aspects of sales and marketing for your business, but first, let's start with some basics.

Here are four questions to ask yourself:

1. How Am I Going To Find New Clients?

_____

_____

_____

2. How Will I Market And Sell My Products/Service?

_____

_____

_____

3. How Will I Build A Customer Base?

_____

_____

_____

4. How Will I Generate Repeat Business?

_____

_____

_____

When it comes to generating sales, I like to break this down into four different sections, which I have displayed visually below.

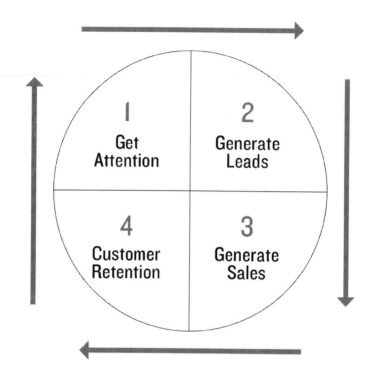

Sales are the lifeblood of any business and can be complicated, so I want to break it down for you into three simple sections:

Objectives

Setting sales targets, and having measurable goals and metrics with defined KPIs, is extremely important when it comes to sales. Think about how you can achieve your objectives.

Tactics

Define the sales process needed to achieve your business objectives. Each business model has different methodologies; what's yours? How do you approach your prospects and then convert them into raving fans? And, lastly, what tools do you need to make this happen? (I will be answering this for you in Chapter 5).

Results

After going through all the hard work of setting objectives and working hard to achieve them, it will all be for nothing unless you measure your success.

Think about the following two questions:
1. What did you want?
2. What did you get?

Once you have the answer to both of them, you can then tweak what works and remove what doesn't.

Now that you have a helicopter view of what you want to achieve as a business, let's get into the specifics around your marketing.

There are seven core aspects to preparing your marketing.

Objectives
What do you want to achieve as a business? What goals are you going to set, and are you going to achieve them? I would like you to write down three objectives on the opposite page.

Products/Services
What are you selling? It is so important that you truly understand your value proposition, and the products/services you are selling. List your products/services on the worksheet.

Pricing
Do you have a pricing structure in place? Think about how you can reward repeat customers by offering them a discount. I will always offer a discount to my audience, and make sure that I am clear with the pricing around my products/services.

Write down how you price your products, and how you offer incentives/discounts to loyal customers, or audience members.

Sales Support
What sales support do you have in place? Who manages your sales process, and how are you solving issues for potential customers before they make their purchasing decision?

Promoting
How are you promoting your business? Social Media will not fix a broken business, so it's important that you have a marketing plan in place which covers all avenues of promotion; not just online, but offline too.

Budget
Marketing can be costly, so it is so important that you have a budget in place so that you are not overspending in certain areas. If you are going to run a PPC

(pay per click) campaign, consider how much this will cost you daily. Write down your marketing budget to the right, and break it down into simple sections so that you can easily see individual spend.

Action Plan

An important part of running a business and generating success is actually having an action plan in place. Think about how you are going to promote your business.

Fill in the blanks to the right after reading through the above.

COMPLETE THE 7 KEY METRICS TO FORM YOUR ONE PAGE MARKETING PLAN

OBJECTIVES	1. What are the specific goals of your business this year?
PRODUCTS & SERVICES	2. What products or services do you offer?
PRICING	3. How will you price your products or services?
SALES & SUPPORT	4. How and where will you sell your products or services?
PROMOTION	5. How will people find out about you and your product?
BUDGET	6. How much do you have to spend on your marketing budget?
ACTION PLAN	7. What will you do and when will you promote and sell your product or service ?

How Are You Promoting Your Business?

There are a number of different ways you can promote your business:

- Website
- SEO
- Blogs
- Press Releases
- Social Media
- Email Marketing
- PPC (Pay Per Click)
- Competitions
- Partnerships
- Leaflets and Posters
- Magazine Adverts.

5. MANAGEMENT AND PERSONNEL

It will take great, decisive leadership to build the best team for your business. You will have to make difficult decisions and establish standards of performance that must be met by every team member. Building an effective team means understanding those around you, knowing their strengths, and, ultimately, what makes them happy in the workplace. Building a team is both an art and a science.

Here are three different ways of doing it. Depending on where your business is and the type of business you run, you will find one of these more suitable than the others.

Employee

An employee is someone you hire to work inside your business and give a specific area to focus on.

Virtual Assistant

A virtual assistant (VA) is someone who is self-employed and provides expertise in administration, technology, creativity (social) or sits in an assistant role from the comfort of their own home. This means you are not responsible for their overheads.

Freelancer

A freelancer is someone who you bring in for a short period to focus on a specific task. They will be experts in their field, and they cost more, but are only there for the short term.

Your Team

This isn't the first time and it definitely won't be the last time I mention how important it is to have the right team around you when building your socially-savvy business. Do you have the right skills to deliver the outcome needed for your Marketing Plan? If not, you will need to hire an agency, or freelancers, or bring in someone to do this for you. You will need a Marketing Management Content Plan, including:

- Social Media Marketing
- Pay Per Click Campaigns
- Search Engine Optimisation
- Website Management
- Writing Articles
- Image Creation
- Marketing Automation
- Email Marketing
- Content Marketing.

Since the launch of Thinkdigitalfirst.com and the expansion of the business, I now have four team members. One works behind the scene keeping things moving through Social Media, and conducting all of the important research. The second manages the community of entrepreneurs and the marketing of the business. My third team member designs all the workbooks, worksheets, cheat sheets, and digital downloads, and the final person manages all of my speaking and training engagements and partnerships.

Each person is on board because of their skillset, and each is as important as the next. My team all work remotely, which means that we all have a great lifestyle that allows us to work without being tied to an office. This was a decision I made early on, as I wanted a successful business that also allows me to be at home with my new family, regardless of whether I'm working from home, or abroad.

6. OPERATIONS AND ASSETS

It's easy to look at the big brands such as Nike or Victoria's Secret and say yes, that is a successful brand, but when it comes to finding your own way as an entrepreneur, branding your business can be challenging. When you develop your branding, you must be authentic, know your values, have your Mission Statement defined and know where you want your business to be in the future.

Building your brand starts with you. Your consumer needs a reason to buy your product or service and that begins with a human connection. Consumers know what they want, and your brand must reflect this. To offer your consumers an engaging experience, your branding needs to reflect this visually. It is critical to have a logo that is recognisable, relatable and consistent with other images. Take a look at your competitors and see how they have defined and visually identified their brands. It is OK to model yourself on the success of the businesses you see every day.

Finding your brand identity does not happen overnight and can be a long, challenging process. You do need to look to the future. Think three years ahead. Will your branding still be relevant to your consumers? As your business goals change, so might your branding; and be aware that consumers are not fond of change, so bear in mind that strong branding will still sell your business in years to come.

> " — *what happens* —
> **ONLINE**
> — *stays online* — "

The visual branding of your company should portray how you will connect with your target audience. Your logo and other business images should be included in the branding part of your business. Your website must also be branded consistently with your marketing material and your online profiles. Having a brand Style Guide will give enable consistency and give new members of your team a single point of reference about the brand and a clear and certain image to identify with.

Let's take a closer look at branding, and the colours you use to showcase your business online.

As you can see from the visual, the eight core brand colours have different meanings, and have associations that you need to be aware of as a brand marketing online.

Colours are just one part of your visual brand. You will also need to think about how you use imagery to reflect your brand. What image style will be attractive and relevant to your audience? Modern? Vintage? Minimalist? Whichever it is, the quality of the images you use is important.

Part of creating your brand style guide means analysing your logo, watermark, colour pallet, texture, font theme and decorative elements. As you can see from my brand style guide, I have taken all of these things into consideration when defining my business online.

WK BOOK BRAND GUIDELINES

LOGOS

 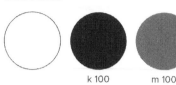

COLOURS

○ ● ●
k 100   m 100
          y 100

CHAPTER NUMBER AND TITLE

ONE

YOU: THERE WILL ONLY EVER BE ONE

#EXPRESSYOURSELF

QUOTE

"SOCIAL MEDIA
—— *will not fix a* ——
BROKEN BUSINESS "

BOOK PAGE HEADERS

THINK #DIGITAL FIRST

FOUR   SETTING UP A SOCIALLY-SAVVY BUSINESS

PAGE NO.

12

FONTS

Proxima Nova
For main body text

KNOCKOUT HTF72 FULLCRUISERWT
For callouts and quotes

KNOCKOUT HTF48 FEATHERWEIGHT
For chapter number, chapter name, page number, page book title,
page chapter heading

KNOCKOUT HTF26 JUNIORFLYWEIGHT
For chapter hashtags

Learning Curve Pro
For quotes

SF BUTTACUP LETTERING SHADED
Only to be used in AOP

AOP SWATCH
For chapter pages

To the left you will see the brand style guide we used to design the book. Over the page is a worksheet for you to fill out around the type of branding you want for your business including logo, colours and fonts.

This is just a starting point for you to know what you would like for your brand, but I have personally always gone to a creative agency to perfect my idea. Find yourself a creative designer, or work with a creative agency to come up with your brand assets.

CREATE YOUR BRAND STYLE GUIDE

Put together branding ideas that represent your brand identity and message.

Brainstorm what you want your logo to look like? E.g. Minimal, Hand-drawn, Line art, Vintage or Heritage?

Consider the colour combinations you may want to use and record the references below?

PRIMARY		SECONDARY	
#	=	#	=
#	=	#	=
#	=	#	=
#	=	#	=
#	=	#	=

Think about what font would suit your brand identity and why? E.g. Upper case, Lower case, Heavy weight, Light weight, Script?

7. FINANCE

When designing the final cost price of your product or service, take into consideration the true cost of acquiring a customer. As a service driven business, your conversion rate might be 50%. This means you have to go through your customer acquisition process twice before you invoice one of those customers. As I previously mentioned, it typically takes eight touch points before a visitor becomes a customer. Let me share with you some things you need to think about when acquiring a customer.

1. You meet at a networking event
2. You connect on LinkedIn and say "hi"
3. You exchange emails
4. They comment on your Facebook Page video
5. You meet up and discuss a mutually beneficial opportunity
6. You retweet a post they published
7. You have a call and agree to move forward
8. Contract signed in a meeting

Every business has a customer acquisition journey and, whichever way you look at it, it will cost you, whether in time or cash – because your time is valuable and has a price. These are some of the actions that either you or your staff have to take before you even deliver on the product or service your business produces. It is important that you value your time and associate a cost with it. This must be part of your final cost price on delivering that service or product.

8. SWOT ANALYSIS

A SWOT analysis will help you identify the positives and negatives inside your business. You identify, measure and analyse your Strengths, Weaknesses, Opportunity and Threats.

Completing a SWOT analysis will help you to:
- improve strategy planning and decision-making;
- determine where change is possible in the business by looking at possibilities and priorities;
- adjust and redefine strategies;
- explore solutions to your customers' pain.

What I would like you to do below is to write down your strengths, weaknesses, opportunities and threats.

COMPLETE A SWOT ANALYSIS OF YOUR CHOSEN BUSINESS

Use the SWOT analysis help sheet to help you discover your business's strengths and weaknesses and any opportunities and threats.

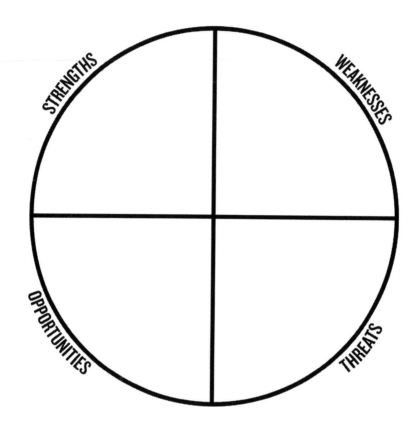

Download our SWOT Analysis template at thinkdigitalfirst.today.

Remember to look at strengths and weaknesses internally and opportunities and threats externally. Internal factors include everything from your staff, location, finances and community reputation. External factors include future trends, the economy, business funding, local and national events, as well as changes in demographics and target market as the business grows.

When I was looking at building my first technology company, I knew what my strengths were and that my 25 years' experience in sales and marketing was where I would excel in the business. What I couldn't provide with my own experience, I knew I needed to bring in with outside help. To build a technology product, I needed an accountant, administrator, web developer and designer in my team. However, this is unique and different for every business.

Really think about where your strengths and weaknesses lie, to help you build the right team around you for the job you need to do, and encourage business growth.

Having launched my second technology business with a focus on education, using a different platform, target audience and business model, I still found that I had weaknesses as an entrepreneur and realised that if these weren't addressed, it would hold the company back from becoming a seven-figure business within three years.

THE ENTREPRENEURS IMPACT PROFILE: ARE YOUR MAXIMISING YOUR IMPACT?

So, what sort of entrepreneur are you? What is your preferred role in terms of making an impact and working with others? Understanding your preferences for working with others will illustrate how you can become the best entrepreneur you can be.

Powered by The GC Index® language and framework, EnSpirit Global have developed The Entrepreneur Impact Profile.

The Entrepreneur Impact Profile is made up of five key roles:
- The Game Changer: transforms the future
- The Strategist: maps the future
- The Implementer: builds the future
- The Polisher: creates a future to be proud of
- The Play Maker: orchestrates the future

This tool helps entrepreneurs to understand how they make their game changing impact and what additional skills are needed in their team to achieve business success.

The Profile will tell you what sort of entrepreneur you are and how you like to make your impact.

By determining which of the 10 Entrepreneur Impact Profiles is your closest match it becomes possible to develop the team you most need around you. The combination of your highest scores from the five roles above determines what kind of entrepreneur you are.

The Entrepreneur Impact Summary Profiles are:

1. Contemporary Entrepreneur: pursues opportunities that build and develop ecosystems.
2. Visionary Entrepreneur: pursues opportunities that challenge the status quo.
3. Traditional Entrepreneur: pursues opportunities that improve services and products within conventional markets.
4. Charismatic Entrepreneur: pursues activities that bring high performance teams together, to create change in the way things operate.
5. Innovative Entrepreneur: seeks opportunities that develop product and services that break convention.
6. Pragmatic Entrepreneur: has a clear sense of what people 'want to buy'.
7. Empowering Entrepreneur: feels most comfortable in the world of social enterprise.
8. Inspirational Entrepreneur: 'raises the bar' of performance, striving to be the 'leading edge' in all they do.
9. Creative Entrepreneur: excels in finding alternative solutions to problems, ones that seem impossible to solve to the naked eye.
10. Aspirational Entrepreneur: uses past learnings to pivot on ideas, to create a better future.

THREE

PROTECTING YOUR TIME TO FOCUS ON SALES

CHAPTER 3

One thing I've learnt in last three years since first writing this book, and using this chapter as a mantra for everything I do on a daily, weekly or monthly basis, is the impact it's had on my life.

Making the decision to have a 'lifestyle' where my work and family are one and not a work/life balance, has meant that I've not only had to value my time (not to every 30 minutes but every 10 minutes) but also my organisation (me and my team) as well as my personal commitments. Something I've taken away from this is the knowledge of how my energy shifts throughout the day.

The way I was working three years ago is very different to today. My energy levels are at their optimum before the afternoon, any time from 5am to 3pm, so when it comes to being creative, managing my team and speaking to new channel partners; this is my 'prime time'. The less important tasks such as admin and emails all come later in the afternoon.

"ARE YOU
— *a* —
BUSY FOOL?"

As an entrepreneur, you're always going to be busy. The question is, are you a busy fool? This is an industry term used to describe someone who is doing a lot of things, but not owning their time or growing their business.

I am passionate about this step in the process of building a successful business because this was where I was in 2008. It wasn't until I began working with my mentor that I really started to build my personal brand and grow my businesses. He shared with me some simple and really effective techniques, which helped me to own my time and stay focused on what I wanted to achieve - and you can do it too.

It's critical to understand where you're spending your time. Here is a document to help you. It will inform what you should be doing every 30 minutes of your waking day. Using this document will give you clarity and focus and a deeper understanding of where you spend your time.

		Monday	Tuesday	Wednesday	Thursday	Friday
	09:00	To do list	Social Media	Social Media	Social Media	Social Media
	09:30	Preparation				
	10:00	Social Media				
	10:30	Social Media				
	11:00	Emails				
	11:30	Sales Call				
	12:00	Sales Call				
	12:30	VA Call				
	13:00	Lunch				
	13:30	Lunch				
	14:00	Marketing				
	14:30	Marketing				
	15:00	Emails				
	15:30	Travel to meeting				
	16:00	Meeting				
	16:30	Meeting				
	17:00	Travel back to office				
	17:30	Debrief from Meeting				
	18:00	Preparation				

ADD YOUR ACTIONS HERE

Download our Time Management Spreadsheet at thinkdigitalfirst.today.

Time management is something many successful, busy entrepreneurs struggle with. If this is you, I'm going to share with you some tips to help you better manage your time. Further on in this book, there are also some tools you can use to protect your time.

When it comes to your working day, remember to spend some time planning. To save time, you will need to spend time, and it's OK to do that, especially if it means your days are more organised. Remember the Pareto Principle, which states that 80% of your success will come from 20% of your focused activity. Work out what that 20% of your focused activity is that drives your 80% success, so you know to give priority to those activities.

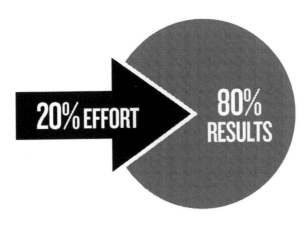

It can be hard to let go and allow others to help you complete tasks, but you'll need to do this if you have a lot on your plate. Delegate the less important tasks and those that are not aligned to your strengths to others in your business, and outsource where possible. Sometimes, things come up that cannot be avoided and it's not the end of the world if this happens. Make sure the most important tasks are completed before anything else, so that if you have interruptions, you know the important things have been accomplished.

This is a great visual analogy. Imagine three empty glass tubes in front of you; the first is empty; the second contains small rocks; and the third has big rocks. How can you get the contents of tubes 2 and 3 into tube 1?

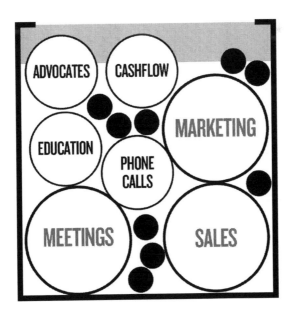

This is where the term "get your big rocks in first" comes from. Once you have all the big rocks in the tube, the small rocks (smaller tasks) can fit around the important tasks (big rocks).

Having deadlines will prevent tasks from dragging on too long. When I know I have a lot to get done in one day, I will always set myself a deadline so I push myself to finalise what needs to be completed. We are not robots, we are human beings, and we can't work 24 hours, 7 days a week. Knowing your limits between work and free time is very important too. Without living a balanced life, what was once work that you enjoyed becomes a chore.

Did you know that when you're concentrating it takes 23 minutes to recover from every interruption? What is your biggest source of distraction? A big one of mine when I'm trying to complete an important task is my mobile phone. I, like many millions in the world, feel uncomfortable being separated from my smartphone. However, I've learnt that by removing this distraction I accelerate moving forward with my daily tasks.

YOUR PRIME TIME

When are you most focused during your working day? Your prime time is the time when you are most proactive in completing important tasks. This could be in the morning, around lunchtime, or in the evening. Make sure you attend to important tasks during the time you are feeling your best, at your highest. Allocating appropriate time to each of these areas is about breaking old habits and forming new ones.

These five tips can help you improve your time and energy management.

1. Scheduling

I find it so important to schedule my day, so that I know when I can take breaks, and when I need to be focused. I base my scheduling on when I'm most productive (which I have already spoken about).

2. Double Your Break Time

When you go to step away from work, and you say to yourself "I'll just take 10 minutes then I'll get back to it", double it. If you feel you need to take a break, it means that your body and mind are telling you to do so, so make sure that you give yourself extra time so that you're more focused when you get back to your work.

3. Speak To Family And Friends

You may find that being in contact with friends and family members will help you take the break you need, and focus on something different.

4. Brainstorm

When you are looking for some R&R, think about brainstorming what you want to do. If you go with the first thought that comes into your head, it is likely coming from desperation rather than what you actually want to do. If you're going to take the time away from your hectic life, make it worthwhile.

5. Break Your Goals Down

If you're setting yourself goals, make sure they are measurable, but also broken down into small chunks. This way, they seem less daunting. Always make sure to reward yourself when you do reach a goal, so that you're more motivated to continue.

We are now going to consider other important areas within your business. Ask yourself how many of the tips below you are following, and if they aren't within your skill set or not a high priority task, are you delegating them to staff members or VAs?

As an entrepreneur we wear lots of different hats. Each of these different hats needs to be a part of your weekly habit. The amount of time you spend on them must be focused and dedicated.

THE DIFFERENT HATS OF A BUSINESS OWNER

The lines between sales and marketing have become blurred because of the way we now communicate online and use digital technology. Therefore the need for clarity in business is even more important.

Sales

Sales are always the lifeblood and pumping heart of any business. To focus on sales, you must have a very clear Go to Market Strategy. This will share your business USP in the right way, from day one, to the right target audience.

When was the last time you did your due diligence to find your business three new customers?

Or more importantly, when did you upsell or cross sell current customers/clients? An astounding 82% of customers have left a company because of a bad customer service experience. Once you have found your prospects, are you taking them through what is called the Customer Acquisition Journey?

This is about creating a process to enable your business to become a well-oiled machine that continuously brings in prospects through your marketing funnel into your sales process.

This is my five step R.E.N.S.A business model (Which I will talk about in Chapter 6):

Step 1: **R**elevancy
Step 2: **E**ngage with your prospects
Step 3: **N**urture your prospects
Step 4: Make the **S**ale
Step 5: Retain and build brand **A**dvocates

While I was looking to acquire Channel Partners for Thinkdigitalfirst.com, or helping a business owner as a coach, I had to protect my time. This includes understanding how many 30-minute calls you need to make followed by how many 60-minute meetings you need to have to acquire one customer. Out of every three phone calls, you might have two meetings, and acquire one customer. If this is true to your business, you know that your ratio is at 3:1 (three phone calls = one customer).

"99% OF VISITORS DON'T BUY
because
BUSINESS OWNERS CAN'T SELL "

The global conversion of visitors to customers is 1%, so if you have 1,000 visitors to your website every month, you will get 10 customers; this is a good KPI for you to focus on. Remember this is an average, meaning many businesses convert much lower and big brands convert at three or four times that.

Determining this will help you understand the value of your time and your true worth. Once you have acquired a customer; what is the lifetime value of this customer? You need to know how much total cost and time you have spent acquiring that customer and working with that customer from the beginning to the end. This will help you calculate your customer's worth and how much your time is worth.

Do you market research your competitors and benchmark their pricing structure against yours?

"FIND YOUR MICRO-NICHE
— *and* —
INCREASE YOUR WORTH„

Marketing

A great analogy I heard about the difference between sales and marketing was:

"Marketing is about bringing the prospect to your front door, and Sales is about opening the door, inviting them in, and keeping them."

Your role as a marketeer is to connect with as many prospects as possible and this is done through offline and online tactics. As a modern day entrepreneur, you must Think #Digital First. For example, when you are wearing your marketing hat and going to a networking event, do your market research to determine who you want to spend your time with and connect with them online before you arrive through various social networks, (my favourites are Twitter and LinkedIn). This is a great way to open a conversation and start a new business relationship. Start by talking about your passion for helping people, and remember you don't need to put yourself into sales mode in the first 30 seconds, because you have already built rapport online.

Some of the best businesses with massive growth in the last 5-10 years are those which have been creative in their marketing and brand positioning. You can model their success, making it your own, by being transparent and bringing your personality and business vision to your marketing strategy.

Taking on the marketing role in your business means you'll have to spend time building relationships offline and online with your potential and existing customers/clients, whether they are direct customers or acquired via a Channel Partner. Keeping consistent with your brand message and online voice is crucial.

I'm not going to spend much time on this as I'll be taking you through a step-by-step process and giving you tips to help you walk before you run (but as a fast growth business) in Chapter 6. I will be taking you through the exact process that generates thousands of prospects and multiple six figure businesses.

Finances

Managing your finances can be difficult if you don't have a background in this field of expertise. Having happy customers who are prepared to pay for your product is great. However, if you don't understand your P&L (profit and loss) you won't know where you stand with your business finances. To the right is a simple 12-month cashflow forecast for you to plug your numbers into.

CASH FLOW FORECAST - 12 MONTHS

Month:	Pre Start	1	2	3	4	5	6	7	8	9	10	11	12	Totals
Receipts														
Cash Sales														£0
Collections from credit sales														£0
New equity inflow														£0
Loans received														£0
Other														£0
Total Receipts	£0	£0	£0	£0	£0	£0	£0	£0	£0	£0	£0	£0	£0	£0
Payments														
Equipment														£0
Payments to suppliers														£0
Staff wages														£0
Rent														£0
Utilities														£0
Insurance														£0
Travel														£0
Telephone														£0
Postage														£0
Office supplies														£0
Advertising														£0
Marketing/promotion														£0
Bank charges														£0
Miscellaneous														£0
Directors' salaries														£0
Loan repayments														£0
Other														£0
Total Payments	£0	£0	£0	£0	£0	£0	£0	£0	£0	£0	£0	£0	£0	£0
Cashflow Surplus/Deficit (-)	£0	£0	£0	£0	£0	£0	£0	£0	£0	£0	£0	£0	£0	£0
Opening Cash Balance	£0	£0	£0	£0	£0	£0	£0	£0	£0	£0	£0	£0		
Closing Cash Balance	£0	£0	£0	£0	£0	£0	£0	£0	£0	£0	£0	£0		

Month:	Pre Start	1
Receipts		
Cash Sales		
Collections from credit sales		
New equity inflow		
Loans received		
Other		
Total Receipts	£0	£0

85

Accountability for cashflow is something every entrepreneur needs to take on board as a responsibility of running a business. Knowing what your burn rate is (monthly expenses: office space, staff costs, travel costs, stationery) gives you the knowledge to focus on bringing in sales to the business to make it profitable. If you don't know what your true costs are in a business, how much time do you know to give yourself to focus on sales?

Operations

How technically-minded are you?

The only three areas of growing your business you need to focus on in terms of managing operations are:

1. Organic Traffic
2. Paid Traffic
3. Partnerships

Each of these requires a different skillset and must be applied at different times.

Your website is your shop window and should be the focal point of everything you do online. If you sell products online, having a transactional website is a must. But even as a service driven business, your website must tell your story and build trust with your visitors. In Chapter 5 I will share my favourite websites for helping to you to achieve your business goals.

Organic and paid traffic can come from the same place (i.e Google) but the ways they work are very different. Organic traffic requires keywords on your website from day one, so Google knows what you do and who your potential clients are. This is free, whereas paid is only financially viable if you have a well converting website and can track and measure your results.

Building a relationship with an organisation which has your ideal customer takes time and perseverance. Sometimes it can take more than 12 months from your initial contact. If your business is not seen to be growing online and offline, this relationship with a new partner might never start.

Maintaining a website; daily use of social media and digital marketing; and understanding Google are three important technical aspects of running a business that you, or one of your team members, needs to be expert at. Remember, your time is priceless. If you're doing something technical that will take you two hours when someone more experienced will only take 20 minutes, your time is better spent elsewhere.

Another part of maintaining your website, along with managing the marketing content, is the copywriting. If you're responsible for this, you automatically become the copywriter for your business, which is time-heavy. Do you have the ability to work at the speed needed for copywriting, as well as the accuracy? Think about this, seriously.

These days, copywriting is integral and the average online content marketing spend should be a minimum of 30% of your overall marketing budget, whatever size your business. If you're an online business it should be up to 80%. This is why having a copywriter who understands the tone of your business is the future of business online.

If you want to be responsible for all the copywriting on your website, marketing and sales materials, you will lose a lot of time, which could be better spent elsewhere to bring in the money. I know that copywriting is not my expertise, so I've brought someone into my business who has the particular knowledge needed, at a small cost.

There are some great websites you can use to find experienced freelance copywriters for a reasonable price, if you don't have the experience or confidence to do it yourself. See Chapter five.

Delegation

As a business owner, delegation is something that cannot be avoided. The appointment of a responsibility to another team member is how I define delegation. Successful people start with a core skills set, like Sales. Evolving into an entrepreneur and building a team is about creating the right atmosphere and learning to manage different personalities. The art of delegation comes from being a great manager. Excelling in Sales doesn't mean you know how to manage five members of staff.

To work well with your team, you need to understand the strengths and weaknesses of each team member. As the founder of your business, you need to be a team leader who has the ability to divide tasks between your team, so the most qualified people in each expertise area are doing the right work. Clever hiring from day one will have you standing on strong foundations for fast business growth.

Choose what tasks you want to delegate. You should be spending your time on the most critical tasks of your business, not ones that can be easily delegated to other team members. If something doesn't interest you, you don't have to do it. Part of building and working with a team is understanding how to work together productively. This also includes online meetings with virtual staff and face-to-face meetings with people who work in your business full or part-time. Their progress is, ultimately, your progress, and because you're not with them in an office every day, you need to stay up-to-date with their daily workings.

"DOES EACH STAFF MEMBER *generate* x3 TIMES THEIR SALARY?"

When delegating, you need to give clear instructions. Spend some time doing this with your team so they fully understand the task at hand. The idea is to save you, as the business owner, as much time as possible, so if you're spending too much time hand-holding, you should pass the task on to someone else. In Chapter 5 I speak about a great online tool that will help you manage this.

You will come across challenges in the workplace every single day, and if you've already built a strong teamwork foundation, your working environment can act as a support mechanism for staff members. It's crucial to build a team that works well together and supports each other.

At one of my start-up companies, we had a 'Stand Up Scrum' (an interactive and incremental agile software development framework for managing product development) once a day. At the start of the working day, I could hear from each member of my team regarding the work they were doing and how they were finding it. We could discuss ideas to move forward and, come to a collective decision around certain areas of the business we all agreed on. Working as a team is critical to your success, because a happy team is a money-making team.

How are you going to work collaboratively with your team? In Chapter 5 I'll share with you some amazing collaborative tools so that you can use to work with your team in a more productive and collaborative way.

Finally, setting a deadline; this is crucial for getting a task completed in a timely manner. Your team need guidance and a part of this includes knowing when a project or task needs to be finished. Make sure you are there for your team when delegating, in case they have any questions only you can answer.

Brand Ambassador

The last hat you need to be able to wear, and in my opinion one of the most important, is being your own brand ambassador.

Entrepreneurs can sit in their comfort zone hiding behind the business. Being in business for the last 25 years has taught me that businesses come and go. Companies reinvent themselves. Stock markets crash. New ways to market your business evolve. The one thing that stays constant throughout your life is you. You are the one that learns and grows from the failures and successes in your personal and business career. As I touched on in Chapter 1, you are the most important part of your business, and at this stage, if there is no YOU, there is no business.

You need to have passion for, and knowledge of, every part of your business. While you may not, for example, be responsible for the technology or financial parts, you are responsible for who is, and you need to know they are doing their job to the best of their ability.

Taking on this role means you might have to stand up in front of a room of 40+ people and talk passionately and informatively about your business. Can you do this? Being confident enough to speak professionally, and to lead your team and build relationships, is what makes a great brand ambassador. It may take time to build these qualities. It is time well spent.

Look at all the hats you need to wear as a business owner: how many of them can you delegate to a member of your team, so you can save your time and focus on bringing in new clients?

A process that works for me, day-in day-out, is assigning tasks such as the first touch point in the process of speaking to a new customer to my Virtual Assistant. When someone is interested in speaking with me about how I can help their business grow, I will get my VA to pre-qualify and book in a 30-minute discovery call with the potential client. After I have taken this call, if I know I can help this individual with their business I arrange a one-hour meeting face-to-face. At the end of that meeting we determine whether we will work together.

Managing clients and customers can be difficult, especially when you're balancing your time spent with them while doing everything else you need to do to keep your business growing.

Here are some ways to help you protect your time:

1. keep a to-do list;
2. always make notes from each client meeting;
3. set achievement goals for your time with each client;
4. hold the meeting and manage distractions;
5. remember not to overwhelm your clients too much;
6. time-manage every client meeting.

Time management is an integral part of building a successful business. While some people may find it easier to focus on just one task at a time, I've come across many people in my industry who think they can multitask extremely well. Before we move onto Chapter 4, I want to talk about multitasking and how it can be used effectively for your time management.

THE ART OF MULTITASKING

Surprisingly, multitasking does have its benefits. However, there is bad multitasking, and there is good multitasking. For example, when driving, you should not let your mobile phone distract you, although listening to the radio or talking to the passenger in a car is deemed OK. All of these have the potential to cause a car crash. However, we have adapted to multitasking, which allows us to do two (or maybe more) tasks at once.

Our brains can handle multiple tasks and it is not dangerous to divide our consciousness. The risk only comes into play when our cognitive resources have too much of a demand - known as the cognitive load. This happens when a task is too severe or time consuming and our ability to perform this task and others at the same time will suffer.

Protecting your time can be difficult. However, with the right tactics you can ensure you are being efficient with your time. Being focused on a task with a deadline and multitasking is not an option. The more focused you are, the better job you will do and the quicker you will achieve your goal.

"STAY FOCUSED

—*get the task finished*—

AND MOVE ON "

One of the best ways to protect your time is to stay away from emails. They can, at times, become a black hole where you lose hours of your precious time. To avoid being sucked in, remember not to look at your emails until you have completed your important tasks. If you're struggling to do this, set a timer so you only spend, say 10 minutes going through emails. Another way to stay time efficient is to keep a checklist of your daily tasks. Doing this, combined with knowing your limits and not multitasking important tasks, will help you focus on sales, while protecting your time.

FOUR

BUILDING YOUR BUSINESS FOR FAST GROWTH

CHAPTER 4

"CONTENT
is the
REASON SEARCH BEGAN IN THE FIRST PLACE"

Welcome to the new world of connecting with your consumers online.

Since August 2013, we have seen Google introduce nine, yes, nine algorithm updates, which have all heavily impacted the way your business will be ranked on Google. Rather than share with you every update (we could be here for a while) here are the most recent changes from Google that have impacted the way I use Google for my business.

Pigeon
The introduction of the Pigeon algorithm came into effect in July 2014. The update provided a more useful and relevant set of local search results that were visible within both Google Maps, and through Google Web search results. Location-based businesses were most affected by this algorithm update. In December 2015, Google introduced the Pigeon algorithm to the UK, Canada and Australia.

Panda 4.2
Similar to the Penguin 3.0 update, Panda 4.2 had little impact and was dubbed as being no more than a 'data refresh'. Panda 4.2 came into action in July 2015.

RankBrain
In October 2015, Google released their RankBrain algorithm. The new learning machine is based on artificial intelligence and helps Google process its search results.

Penguin 4.0
Let's take a closer look at Penguin 4.0, the most recent confirmed update to the Google Algorithm. Penguin 4.0 was announced on the 23rd September 2016 as a real-time, core algorithm. The main rollout of the first phase of Penguin 4.0

was on the 27th September 2016 and marked the rollout of the new algorithm which devalued bad links instead of penalising websites.

AdWords Shakeup

Google announced major changes to AdWords in February 2016. They removed right-column ads entirely, and introduced 4-ad top blocks on commercial searches. Whilst this would only affect businesses paying for AdWords, it still impacted CTR (click through rates) for both paid and organic search results.

Possum

While the Possum update was unconfirmed by Google, SEO experts noted a huge change in search results. This change took place in September 2016 and only impacted the Local Finder (local results/Google Maps). The purpose of this update was to diversify local results, and prevent spam from ranking. This was the biggest local update since Pigeon in 2014.

Google is known for consistent algorithm updates, which on one hand is great, but on the other is difficult to keep up with.

There has however, as I am writing this book, been a new 'unconfirmed' major algorithm update which is going by the name Fred. Fred has reportedly hit low-valued content sites aimed at revenue generation rather than connecting with their consumers through the content they share. It is now more important than ever to create content that is more than just a way of driving traffic.

FUTURE-PROOFING

As we move through Chapter 4, you'll see a huge focus on one specific aspect of growing a business that I believe to be key, and that's future-proofing. Whilst we are still getting your business ready online, I'll be giving you an in-depth understanding of each piece of the online marketing puzzle, and how you can win new business as a thought leader.

Before we move from algorithms to Search Engine Optimisation (SEO), I want to talk about the user-journey on your website. We have evolved into the 'experience economy' and have to give our customers an experience they fall in love with.

A clean, simple, fast and effective onsite experience, often called a user-journey, can be broken down into two important factors.

Firstly, the User Experience (UX), which is about how the user feels when they explore many different approaches to solving a specific user problem. The broad responsibility of the UX is to ensure the user flows logically from one step to the next. One way a UX might do this is by conducting in-person user tests to observe behaviour. By identifying content and visual stumbling blocks, you can refine your search to create the best user experience.

Secondly, unlike UX, which is concerned with the overall feel of the product, the User Interface (UI) is all about how the product is laid out. It's the design of each screen or page that a user interacts with and it ensures that the UI is visually communicating the path a UX has laid out.

To help you get a better understanding of this, ask yourself this. What do I want a user to do? Also, how do I want to communicate with them? Is it by capturing their name or email, or by getting them to buy your product or service? If you're still not clear, take a look at what your competitors are doing and go through the step-by-step process yourself. If you are finding this difficult, so will your user.

Now let's take a look at how to futureproof your business through Search Engine Optimisation (SEO).

SEO is all about making sure your online presence is visible to those who are most likely to need your product or service. Understanding your business, target market and product/service is the foundation for marketing your business through online content using keywords.

When I first wrote this section, there were certain aspects of SEO that were more important than others. This has now completely changed and whilst keywords are still important to help define your business, the way you create your SEO needs to be done through talking to your customers, and thinking about how THEY search for what your business has to offer online.

SEO can be broken down into two types: Onsite and Offsite. With Google reaching over 1.2 trillion searches yearly, you need to stand out as a business and one of the best ways to do this is by having a great SEO strategy in place both for your onsite, and offsite SEO.

SEO ONSITE

Onsite is optimisation within your website and includes domain name, meta description, web content, internal links, title tags and keywords, rich media files, permalinks, outbound links, bounce rate and loading speed, to name a few.

You want to be at the top of the Google search engine as a result of using the right keywords. The higher you are on the search, the more likely you are to make sales. To continue telling the story, you need to make sure every page on your website is optimised from a search engine perspective, otherwise your website will lose potential sales.

Because of all the latest updates from Google, the way you define your keywords has changed, and the two main differences are around using long-tail keywords (rather than just one word keywords) and understanding the way your customers think. If you want targeted and niche traffic, this is the best route to go. Whilst you may see some of your traffic drop when changing your keyword structure this will be because you are getting more targeted, and those who do visit your website are actually interested in your product/service.

On-page SEO has always been a huge part of my SEO strategy as I understand how key this is. If you have great on-page SEO, you can get a first page Google Ranking, if done properly. On-page SEO can be broken down into 4 sections; general, optimising content, performance changes and URL optimisation.

General
This is where all of the basic on-page SEO should be looked at. Start with adding an XML sitemap, navigation, robots.txt file, an SEO plug-in for your website (I use Yoast) and fixing the webmaster tools. You should then look at the SEO for all of your web pages including meta tags, meta description and titles.

Optimising Content
After you have gone through the 'general' process, you need to look at all of your existing website content. This is where you will make changes to your content. You should be looking at things like duplicate content, visual design, media usage, keywords, internal linking, bounce rate, CSS, outbound linking and new content.

Performance Changes
You need to optimise your website to make sure it's mobile friendly, with good loading speed and hosting. Use tools such as Google PageSpeed Insights and WP Rocket (for WordPress).

URL Optimisation
Having a good URL structure will impact both your rankings, and how well your users will be able to recall your content. Aim for memorable URLs, use 301 redirects where necessary and use your keywords to define your content.

SEO OFFSITE
Offsite SEO is link building. Search engines will quantify a website's influence online based on what other online sources say about the site, which is where link building comes in. Along with link building, there are three other parts to offsite SEO you need to implement.

Link Building
A link building campaign objective should be to have inbound links to your website from high quality and popular sources. Having quality links with

regularly updated content are two sure fire ways to rank high in the search engines and drive more traffic to your website.

Competitor Analysis

There is no one better to learn from than your competitors. Analysing the way your competitors are doing their SEO will help you learn a great deal about your own business, whether this is through success or failure. Doing this will help you achieve the right outcome when developing your online marketing strategy. Looking at everything from their site architecture, keywords and inbound links will give you the knowledge you need to improve your own infrastructure.

Website Code

Coding constructs a website, and this is an important factor you need to consider when doing your SEO. The better the layout of the website and the easier the code is to read, the higher Google will rank you in their search.

Analytics

You must monitor the performance of your website. Without doing this, you won't be able to see how much traffic you're getting, sales you're receiving and many other important analytical factors. Running a regular analytical performance report will provide you with the data you need, and I will give you a tool to do this in the next chapter.

Onsite and offsite SEO are very important steps in building a socially-savvy business, because without the correct SEO data on your website and link building in place, Google especially, won't rank your business higher than your competitors.

GOOGLE KEYWORD RESEARCH FOR SEO

To make sure you're building the right keyword strategy for your business, you need to either hire someone to help you do this, or learn from an expert and do it yourself. The best tool for your SEO research around your business and target customer as a first step is Google Adwords: Keyword Planner. This Google tool allows users to build a document based on keywords around their business and, based on monthly searches, see how influential those keywords will be for your business.

To give you an example; one of my clients is a bespoke furniture maker with different types of products, including: cabinets, taps, fitted kitchens, bedroom furniture and more. Together we created an excel document with one tab labelled target customers and a further four tabs for each different product range.

We researched the industry, looked at how potential customers were searching for the products and created the excel spreadsheet with a breakdown of this data.

SEO RESEARCH

Phrases	Keywords 1	Keyword 2	Keyword 3
Cabinet Making	Kitchen cabinets	Cabinet Design	kitchen cabinet designs
Cabinet Makers	Cabinet Maker	Bespoke Cabinet Maker	London Cabinet Maker
Kitchen Cabinet Makers	kitchen cabinets	solid wood kitchen cabinets	cabinet maker
Kitchen Cabinet Maker	Cabinet Maker	kitchen cabinet doors	solid wood kitchen cabinets
Bespoke Cabinet Makers	cabinet maker	cabinet makers london	Kitchen doors
Bespoke Cabinet Makers London	cabinet makers london	Cabinet Maker London	free standing kitchen cabinets
Bespoke Furniture	Bespoke Furniture London	bespoke furniture makers	fitted wardrobes
Bespoke Kitchen	Bespoke Kitchens	Bespoke Kitchens London	kitchen units
Fhandmade	bespoke kitchens london	designer kitchens	kitchen units
Bespoke Kitchen Company	Bespoke Kitchens	bespoke kitchens london	handmade kitchen company
Bespoke Handmade kitchen	handmade kitchens	bespoke kitchen design	bespoke kitchen
Bespoke English Kitchen	plain english kitchens	Bespoke Kitchens	plain english kitchen
Bespoke English Kitchens	plain english kitchens	Bespoke Kitchens	plain english kitchen
Bespoke London Kitchen	bespoke kitchens london	new kitchen	handmade kitchens
Bespoke London Kitchens	bespoke fitted kitchens london	bespoke kitchens	bespoke kitchen design
Bespoke shaker Kitchen	Bespoke Shaker style kitchens	Shaker Kitchens	shaker style kitchen
Bespoke shaker Kitchens	shaker kitchens	shaker style kitchen	shaker kitchen
Fitted Furniture	fitted bedroom furniture	fitted bathroom furniture	fitted wardrobes
Fitted Kitchen	fitted kitchens	fitted kitchens london	Bespoke fitted kitchens
Fitted Kitchens	fitted kitchens uk	kitchen cupboard doors	Fitted Kitchen
Designer Fitted Kitchen	Designer Fitted Kitchen Units	fitted kitchens	designer kitchens
Designer Fitted Kitchens	Designer Fitted Kitchen Units	fitted kitchens	designer kitchens
Marylebone Cabinet Makers	london marylebone	cabinet maker	quality kitchens
Marylebone Kitchen	natural kitchen marylebone	marylebone london	kitchen london
Marylebone Kitchens	handmade kitchens	bespoke kitchens	kitchen fitters
Marylebone designer Kitchens	designer kitchens	handmade kitchens	luxury kitchen designs
Marylebone kitchen designer	kitchens by design	kitchens direct	kitchen designers london
Marylebone designer kitchen company	handmade kitchen company	fitted kitchens	luxury kitchens

Download our SEO research Template at thinkdigitalfirst.today.

You can do the same for your business so it is accurately described through keywords and then you can move on to plan your website page map (the user journey you want to send your customers on when they come to your website home page). You want to be looking for keywords which have low competition with high monthly search.

As soon as you've created an excel document for your business with at least 50 keywords for each tab, you can apply the data to your website and tell your own website story. If you're new to SEO and don't know what information you should be putting where on a basic level, keep reading.

Here is a Step-by-Step guide to preparing the right keywords to add to your website, which will also prepare you for content marketing your brand online.

1. Download my Keyword Research Template from www.thinkdigitalfirst.com
2. Sign up for Google Keyword Planner. When going through this process, it will ask you to create an ad campaign – which you will need to do to

access this tool. Make sure that once you've done this, you pause the campaign so you don't get charged.

3. It will ask you what you would like to do; click 'search for new keyword and ad group ideas'.

4. You are given a few options. I recommend taking the URL of a competitor and placing it into the 'your landing page' box and click 'get ideas'. This will give you a comprehensive list of keywords and phrases used on their website and used by an individual to search for the product/service. This is a great starting point, where you can take the keywords relevant to your business and place them in the keyword spreadsheet.
   a. Start with the word chosen
   b. Then the adgroup
   c. Take three words that appear in the adgroup (always making sure you are only taking the relevant keywords and phrases)

5. Continue to populate the Keyword spreadsheet using different tabs for:
   a. The business: an overview of what the business does
   b. The target customer: list all the attributes of a target customer
   c. Your specific products or services

6. Remember to add the amount of monthly searches along with how popular that keyword is.

You should now have an excel spreadsheet which is full of keywords that are all relevant to your business.

The next step is to take this information and define the metadata and page copy for each word and every page of your website, including your 'About' and 'Contact Us' pages.

To make sure you are staying page specific, you must decide which four keywords you want to stay consistent with for Google (metadata) and the consumer (on-page copy).

Here is an example.

KITCHEN CABINET MAKER	Focus phrase	Kitchen Cabinet Maker
	Alt Img Text	Kitchen Cabinet Maker
	SEO Title	[BUSINESS NAME] I London Based Bespoke Kitchen Cabinet Maker
	Meta description	As a kitchen cabinet maker, we are dedicated to quality and elegance when creating our bespoke, hand-crafted kitchens.
	Landing Page Copy	For the best bespoke kitchen furniture, come down to our London-based Marylebone store for a wide selection of designer cabinets, and fitted kitchens. We are open six days a week for all of your kitchen cabinet maker needs, and will offer you a unique, one-to-one service that is tailored to your specific kitchen needs.

Download our SEO Meta Data Template at thinkdigitalfirst.today.

Once you've completed the all-important pages of your website in this format, you need to go and apply it to the rest of your website. Remember to go to Google Webmaster and inform Google you've made changes to your website, so it can crawl and index all your new keywords.

In Chapter Six, I will share with you how to take these keywords and apply them to your content marketing strategy and integrate it into your digital communication, staying brand and keyword consistent.

SOCIAL NETWORKS

Do you remember how popular MySpace was, and how Bebo revolutionised the way we connected with friends and family online?

Facebook has been around for over a decade now, and the success of 'The Social Network' was like nothing before.

Since writing the original version of this book, so much has changed.

We have seen Vine come and go, Microsoft's acquisition of LinkedIn, Facebook's acquisition of Instagram and Whatsapp, and the growing importance of video and live-streaming.

I have amassed a following of over 100,000 people and have spent thousands of hours helping businesses succeed through the strategic use of Social Media. Part of being an online success and generating sales through Social Media is staying up-to-date with the landscape.

Before we take a closer look at the Social Media landscape, I just want you to think about your approach when it comes to implementing everything I talk about below. Think about YOUR customers, and how everything you can do as a business NOW, will complement everything you want to achieve as a business further down the line.

"CHOOSE THE RIGHT
SOCIAL MEDIA NETWORK
to
ENGAGE WITH YOUR AUDIENCE"

FACEBOOK
Between you and me, I had fallen out of love with Facebook when I first wrote this book, but due to all of the changes that have happened over the last three years, we are now best friends. Let me tell you why.

Facebook now has around 2 billion monthly users.

Here is what is now important when it comes to Facebook.

Facebook has, and always will be 'The Social Network'. It has the largest following, was the first to take social to a whole new level and is always staying as innovative as possible. The biggest issue I find with Facebook is that whilst they are always introducing new features, it can be difficult to understand what they TRULY mean for an average user like me.

Newsfeed
Facebook's news feed has always been the main selling point of the social network and changes are always being made. In late 2016, Facebook announced a minor change that significantly impacted how content will show up in your news feed.

As a user, your Facebook news feed will show you more content from the friends you care about, and less from pages you are following. This means that as a business using Facebook Pages, you will not be able to reach your audience like you used to.

Pages
Whilst Facebook Pages has not been an amazing visitor, lead or revenue driver over the last few years, having a Facebook Page does build trust online, and give your 'fans' a place to interact with you.

Since running a giveaway through Facebook earlier this year, I have built my page following, and have actually fallen back in love with Facebook Pages because I now see an increase in engagement.

For you to get the most out of your Facebook Page, here are some of my top tips.

1. Use Your 'Real' Facebook Personal Account To Create Your Page
Many businesses will create a 'dummy' personal account, to link this to their page so that they can distance themselves from the page. The issue with doing this is that it goes against Facebook's terms of service, and does give them grounds to shut down your Facebook Business Page if you have more than one personal Facebook account.

2. Have An Engaging Cover Photo
Your Facebook Page cover photo is going to be a selling point for your business, so make sure it is engaging for your visitors. I share with you a great tool in the next chapter that will help you create this.

3. Add Descriptions and Links To Your Images
When you upload an image, including your profile picture and cover photo to Facebook, add a link through to your website to encourage visitors to come over to your website and find out more.

4. Add A Call-To-Action Button To Your Facebook Page Cover Photo
Facebook have a feature that allows you to add one of their seven pre-made CTA (call-to-action) buttons to your Facebook Page cover photo. You have the option of 'Sign Up', 'Shop Now', 'Contact Us', 'Book Now', 'Use App', 'Watch Video' and 'Play Game. Make sure you choose the one that is most relevant to your business.

5. Customise Your Facebook Page Tabs
Go to the Facebook App Centre to find relevant apps to add to your Facebook Page. They have a great selection of apps that you can use to promote your business, and once you have chosen them, you can then rearrange the order, and decide how they are shown on your page.

6. Complete Your 'About' Section

It can seem like an obvious step, but I have seen that a lot of businesses do forget about utilising their 'About' section. This is more than just writing a bio about your business.

Take a look at the Milestones feature and add in all of the important milestones around your business so that your audience can see them.

7. Run Live-Streams

I talk about this further on in this chapter, but, for me, live-streams have been the biggest engagement driver inside Facebook this year. If I'm going to do a live-stream inside my Facebook Page, I'll always send an email to my audience first to both increase 'likes' on my page, and so that they can be there in real-time.

8. Have A Healthy Content Balance

Sharing content on a regular basis is a great way to encourage engagement, and I give you templates to help you achieve this in this chapter, and Chapter 6. As well as regular content, you also need to vary the type of content you share.

As great as live-streams and videos are; not all of your audience is going to want to interact with you in this way.

9. Pin Important Posts At Top Of Your Page

Do you 'pin' your important post to the top of your page? As timelines are designed in chronological order, your most recent post will sit at the top of your timeline, unless you manually change this. You can 'pin' one post at a time, and when you do this, make it a post that does talk about an offer, upcoming event, or announcement.

10. Always Measure Your Success

Inside of your Facebook account, you are able to manage all of your Facebook analytics. Stay on-top of your analytics, and always measure for success to understand what is working, and what isn't. I find that Facebook Page Analytics are very insightful, and give me an overview of the engagement inside of my page.

Groups

What I've realised over the last year is how important Facebook Groups are.

For me, it has given my entrepreneurs who have come through my training program a safe and secure place to talk about all of their concerns, issues and problems around growing their business online. This has enabled other entrepreneurs in the group to get involved in the conversation and give their point of view.

I have created a private members' Facebook Group with 500+ members who have supported me through my talks, webinars, challenges, and products/services. This group has changed the way I look at Facebook and, more importantly; has allowed me to build a community of engaged target customers.

Inside Facebook Groups, you can also run live-streams which can be private, and just for your Facebook Group members. I do this on a regular basis to give my audience a chance to ask questions about courses they may be on.

Another great feature inside Groups is being able to upload documents so that everyone has access to them. I encourage my audience to upload their blogs and PDFs around their business to get feedback from me, my team and other group members.

Workplace
This is a brand new feature that allows you to collaborate with your team in a safe, secure and private place. You can connect with all members of your business and turn your ideas into actions. It is a group-like feature with a news feed bringing you up-to-date with all of the latest important tasks taking place.

Inside Workplace, you also have a 'work chat' to automate alerts, speak with colleagues and take care of all of your day-to-day tasks. I have been recently using this with my team, and have found it to be a very effective tool.

Notes
Do you want to publish your articles on Facebook, just like you do on LinkedIn? Notes is a great feature, and one which most businesses are not utilising. You can add a cover image, format your text, resize photos and share your notes with more than just your audience.

If you are going to use notes, consider only sharing part of your article, and linking back to the original post on your website to avoid any penalties around duplicating content.

Advertising
A huge 75% of brands on Facebook will pay for Facebook Ads to promote their business. Facebook are always looking at ways to improve their service, and this is exactly what they have done for their Lead Adverts.

The new features include creative formats, using carousel and video features as well allowing you to provide more detail to potential buyers about the advantages of sharing their information using the new context card. You can use this context card to provide more information, before a user takes the next step.

Also, new to the Lead Adverts functionality is being able to integrate Lead Adverts with your email marketing, or CRM tool. So far, Facebook have integrated with Salesforce, Zapier, Mailchimp, Infusionsoft and various other management tools.

All these updates are a great move from Facebook to make their lead advertising even more appealing to small businesses who rely heavily on Social Media advertising.

Facebook Pixel

If you're looking for something geared towards conversions, rather than generating leads, have a look at Facebook Pixel. This is a piece of code that is embedded into your website and connects to Facebook Ads to tell you the actions people are taking as a result of your ad. If ROI is important to you (and it should be) this is a must-use feature, giving you the ability to run a more efficient advert, with easy to understand analytics.

You can use Facebook's Pixel Tracker to track the activity of your target audience from the moment they click on an ad, easily understand the success of your advertising campaigns, measure ROI and to be more efficient with your budget. Another great feature when looking to advertise on Facebook is Custom Audiences. Custom Audiences are used by uploading your existing database to make an audience that you want to target for a Facebook Ad. Custom Audiences is also available on Instagram. Facebook will take your database and analyse every single person who has used the email on your list to create a Facebook account and target your ads at them.

Live Stream

At the end of 2014, Facebook hosted around one billion video views per day. Facebook now hosts around 8 billion video views per day. The popularity of video consumption is undeniable.

Facebook launched Facebook Live in May 2016, and whilst there was some scepticism from digital entrepreneurs in the beginning, the importance of the feature has not gone unnoticed. Facebook Live is an amazing way to connect with your target audience through the power of not only video, but LIVE video. Real-time interaction is one of the best ways to build an authentic audience, and to tell your story online.

I ran a Social Media Giveaway, and I decided to put the Facebook Live feature to the test. I ran two live videos; the first was during the giveaway to encourage people to enter, and after the giveaway had finished to broadcast the winners. I realised that there was so much power inside Facebook with video, especially with adding text. A huge 80% of Facebook videos are watched without sound.

Live streaming is not only great from a business perspective. When writing this chapter, I jumped on a live stream organised by Mark Zuckerberg, where he films, in real-time, his lunch in his back garden with his friends. How else would I be able to get access to this kind of content?

TWITTER

My favourite social network; Twitter has over 15 million active users in the UK. Over 80% of the 15 million active users access the social network from their mobile, with a further 29% checking their Twitter feed multiple times during the day.

Just like Facebook, a lot has changed inside Twitter.

140-Character Change
Whilst the 140-character limit is still in place, the 'rules' around what counts towards the character limit have changed. This was announced in 2016 and Twitter have now released the news that the 140-character limit is now TRUE to the content you share online as a part of your Twitter marketing. Here is a breakdown of the changes.

You will still only get the 140-character towards text based messages and links, however the following types of content will no longer count towards the character limit;
- Quote Tweets
- GIF's
- Polls
- Videos
- Images

Each of these pieces of content takes up around 23 characters in a tweet, which is around 16% of the 140-character limit. This will now mean you have more valuable space to share your message on Twitter as a part of your Twitter marketing.

Advertising
Twitter has always been seen to be running behind the likes of Facebook and Instagram, but recent changes to their advertisement options have given businesses a great chance of connecting with customers inside Twitter.

Twitter now offers four different objective-based campaign options:

1. Increase Website Traffic
Showcase your business and send your audience to your website.

2. Grow Your Twitter Following
Promote your Twitter account, and your specific tweets to encourage engagement and growth.

3. Maximise Brand Awareness
'Promote' your tweets to give your business a boost in brand awareness.

4. Get People Talking
Similar to option three, you can 'promote' your tweets to generate buzz for your brand on Twitter.

Twitter has also introduced specific ad targeting where you are able to define who you want your ads to go to. You can define this through location, language, gender, interest, device, behaviour, follower count, keywords and geographical location.

If you are looking to run an ad campaign inside Twitter, consider using Twitter cards so that you can attach photos and videos to your tweets to drive traffic back to your website.

Tagging
Did you know that you can upload a photo to Twitter and tag your followers in this photo so that they are notified by Twitter? This has been extremely powerful for me, especially when I ran my Social Media Giveaway.

I noticed that tweets with an image where I had tagged 10 businesses/individuals that I engage with on a regular basis received over 150% more engagement compared to a text-driven tweet.

Lists
The biggest problem with Twitter is noise. Whilst I may follow thousands of people on Twitter, there is no way I could use just Twitter's newsfeed to see what those I follow are saying online. I found a solution years ago and have only recently realised that it isn't as well-known as it should be.

This isn't a new feature of Twitter, but it is still as powerful as ever. For me, Twitter Lists has been one of Twitter's best features.

Creating a Twitter List was my ultimate solution and helped me listen to what was important. Millions of Twitter users have done the same, and with the ability to create 1,000 lists per account, you can take the next step today and get organised.

Polls
At the end of 2015, Twitter announced a brand new feature for all their users: Twitter Polls.

Twitter previously allowed users to ask questions and track their replies within their community through the use of hashtags or asking for 'retweets' or 'favourite' to cast a vote. This new feature allows you to create your own poll straight from your newsfeed for a 24-hour period.

This tool will be invaluable for me, as feedback from my community is crucial for my next steps when it comes to webinars, events, training and new products I want to launch. Do note that you can vote just once on any poll, and this will not be shared publicly.

Twitter TV
Earlier this year, Twitter introduced an always-on, live stream video section of its apps and desktop site. Previously, Twitter had live-streamed events such as The Oscars, and the Presidential Inauguration, but now they have taken it one step further.

Twitter's focus will be to cover news events that are happening worldwide. This is a great move from Twitter, making it the first network to introduce social live-streaming TV.

LINKEDIN
LinkedIn is the largest B2B social network and membership is getting close to the half a billion mark. There are many ways you can use LinkedIn to market yourself and your business.

80% of B2B Social Media leads still come from LinkedIn, and there are still two new LinkedIn users joining every second. The average LinkedIn user spends 17 minutes on the site per month. The power of LinkedIn as a B2B social network is more apparent than ever, especially after being acquired by Microsoft for an incredible $26.2 BILLION.

The first thing you must do is complete your profile up to 'all star', by filling in all your profile sections and getting recommendations. A quick tip: for you to be seen on the first page in the search, you must place two keywords, which reflect who you are and what you do, in five separate places on your LinkedIn profile, as listed below.

1. Professional headline
2. Summary
3. Skills
4. Current job
5. Past job

By doing this, you are visible to LinkedIn's algorithm. You also need to set up a business profile and ask all of your staff, stakeholders, Board members etc. to add their role to their profile. Start a group – getting involved in groups is a great way to connect with like-minded people and reach your target audience.

A lot has changed inside LinkedIn recently, and I am going to share these changes with you now.

New Interface
Yes, LinkedIn has introduced a whole new interface. The way you navigate around it has changed. Let's take a look at the important changes:

Home Page: The way this looks has changed, with a cleaner and simpler layout.

Who's Viewed Your Profile Page: This now has its own tab inside LinkedIn.

Your Activity Page: This is where you can look at status updates, posts and engagement with other LinkedIn members. Through the 'all activity' option, you can now see all your engagement including comments and content engagement.

Articles: This now has its own tab, where, in chronological order, you can see all your published articles.

Your Network: Inside 'My Network' you can see how many connections you have, as well as connection requests.

Notifications: This used to be a dropdown list, but now 'Notifications' has its own separate page.

'Me': Under the 'Me' tab inside your LinkedIn account is a host of new (and previously existing) options for you to explore.

Advertising

I've found that LinkedIn has been the most successful Social Media revenue driver. I use each of the main social networks, as well as Google, to promote my business, but since the beginning of this month LinkedIn has become my NBF (new best friend).

Why?

Because the way I can market to my potential customers has become more effective and intelligent.

At the end of April 2017, LinkedIn introduced a brand new piece of software that allows you to combine LinkedIn's professional data with your own LinkedIn Data to create campaigns that target a specific audience. Matched Audiences will help you engage with the key members of your audience through three different features; Website Retargeting, Account Targeting and Contact Targeting.

Website Retargeting: With website retargeting you can re-engage with your website visitors and nurture them through engagement.

Account Targeting: Account targeting is a unique option where you can upload a list of company names to match against the 12 million LinkedIn company pages. You now have the power to market to thought leaders and decision makers with all the hard work of finding them done for you by LinkedIn's new remarketing feature.

Contact Targeting: For me, contact targeting is the most powerful tool because of the large database that I have. I can now upload this database to LinkedIn through a CSV file and engage with potential customers that have already been through my email marketing funnel.

Sponsored updates allow you to raise awareness for your business and generate quality leads. Publishing content on LinkedIn is a great way to connect to professionals who are already in your network. With sponsored updates, you can reach an even larger audience across multiple channels, including mobile.

TWO WAYS YOU CAN PROMOTE YOURSELF ON LINKEDIN

The way we use Social Media and more specifically LinkedIn has evolved. We, as marketers, can use LinkedIn to push content, and send our connections over to our website. The way we need to market to potential customers is through understanding what they want, and the way they want to receive it. In other words, where they want it.

LinkedIn is more than just a place to find new staff members, connect with work colleagues and find other businesses to help solve a problem you might have. I'm going to share, and show you three different ways you can market your business: through generating organic traffic, (natural visitors to my profile and website every single day) and through paid traffic that drives target users to a specific marketing campaigning I'm running at that moment (I pay LinkedIn for every click through).

So let's get into the difference between organic, and paid marketing as well as giving you my top tips to LinkedIn marketing success.

LinkedIn Pulse

I have over 300 articles on LinkedIn Pulse, and have over 15,500 content followers. LinkedIn Pulse has been an amazing traffic and revenue driver for me, especially over the last five years. It's taken me nine years to mould my personal writing style so that I can stay consistent with the content I share. LinkedIn Pulse is a great place for me to engage with my audience whilst also increasing my presence as a thought leader.

More than a million LinkedIn users have been posting on Pulse, with over 130,000 posts being published every week. One of the best ways you can utilise Pulse is to get featured on their channel. To make this a possibility, use your keywords in the title of the blog, and in the content you create. You can also reach out to them on twitter via @LinkedInPulse and ask them to feature your content in a specific category.

Remember that LinkedIn Pulse is completely free of charge for you to use,.so make sure that every article you write on your website gets re-purposed and shared on LinkedIn Pulse for maximum exposure.

Custom Audiences

At the end of last month, LinkedIn introduced a brand new feature called Custom Audience. I have been testing this tool since it has launched, and have seen that 18% of my webinar signups have been through the use of LinkedIn's InMail Sponsored feature.

The InMail paid feature is a great way to reach your audience's inbox in a more personal and direct way. The reason I decided to do this is that I'm connected with thousands of LinkedIn users, and I can't connect with every single one through the content I share, so spending money and re-engaging with them inside their InMail allows me to give them what THEY want.

You will also find three other features inside Custom Audiences, which can be used as a part of your LinkedIn Marketing; Website Retargeting, Account Targeting and Contact Targeting which I spoke about earlier on in this chapter.

LINKEDIN DOS AND DON'TS

When it comes to LinkedIn etiquette, there are some things that businesses owners need to know. Firstly, LinkedIn cannot be treated like any other social network, because it is a B2B network, being used for professional purposes.

This doesn't mean your approach needs to change completely, though. You still need to be as engaging as you would on other social networks, but there are some helpful tips to follow.

Complete Your Profile

This might sound basic, but I come across so many business owners who have yet to fully complete their LinkedIn profile. LinkedIn makes life really easy by telling you how complete your profile is through a percentage system, and once at 100%, you'll get your 'All Star' status.

Don't Expect Everyone To Network Like You Do

People buy from people, but this doesn't mean that everyone will engage with you in exactly the same way. Some of your audience might engage with you consistently as this is how they want to talk with you. Other potential customers may engage with you only when they feel like it.

When looking at LinkedIn, you do need to be patient and understand that not everyone uses LinkedIn like you do. Not everyone has the time to respond straight away, nor do they want to.

Personalise Connection Requests

When reaching out to someone whom you don't know on a personal basis, but want to build a working relationship with, personalise your connection request. Explain who you are, why you want to connect with them and whether you see an opportunity together. This will make the connection feel more open to accepting the request and opening a dialogue with you.

Avoid Spamming

There are so many ways you can use LinkedIn that don't involve you spamming your LinkedIn community. Don't post attention-seeking updates and don't send friend requests to people you don't know. It's important that your audience trusts you, and spamming will only work against you.

Share Video and Images

Posts with visuals get 14x more views. Get creative, but stay brand consistent with the images you share. Think about infographics and how you can create one that's engaging, whilst also being informative.

PINTEREST

Pinterest launched in 2010, and in seven years has grown active usage to 150 million users. Did you know that 88% of all Pinterest users purchased a product they pinned and a further 49% have purchased five or more products they pinned?

Pinterest has made strides towards becoming one of the most engaging social networks, especially with the introduction of Pinterest Visual Discovery in 2017.

Did you know that when people hear information, they are only likely to remember 10% of that information three days later. Pair this information with a relevant image and people retain up to 65% of the information; that's a 55% increase in recall JUST by using an image.

Pinterest is known for being a very visual social network, and their new tool has most definitely revolutionised the way people search for visual information. Visuals are the way to selling, and Pinterest has understood that to really spend money on something, consumers need to see it with their own eyes. Pinterest has always said that it is "built for open-minded discovery" and the Pinterest Visual Discovery Tool allows you to take online window shopping to a whole new level.

The new discovery tool allows you to search for an image, zoom in and search for that product. How many times have you seen something on Pinterest that you want to buy, but can't seem to find where to buy it online? The new, revolutionised piece of technology from Pinterest allows you to discover products/services without having to leave the platform.

Pinterest has two other revolutionary features; Pinterest Lens and Shop The Look.

Pinterest Lens

Pinterest Lens lets you use a camera in your Pinterest app to discover products based on what you see behind the camera lens.

With this new feature, you can now use the inspiration of the real world and combine it with the digital world to give you an experience which has yet to be created by any other social network.

Shop The Look

Pinterest Visual Discovery Tool now includes a 'Shop The Look' feature. You may be aware of the 2015 introduction of looking at an outfit, and seeing related ideas. Pinterest has taken this one step further.

You can now track the products down, and buy them. This is not just for clothing, you can do it with decor, and any other visual product on Pinterest. Just tap the circle on each item to find where you can buy them from the brand's website, or even inside Pinterest.

Pinterest have teamed up with Curalate, Olapic, Project September, Refinery29 and ShopStyle to bring this feature to the market.

To help you with your marketing on Pinterest, here are seven of my top tips.

1. Keywords

The great thing about Pinterest is that Google LOVES it, and because of this, you must start utilising descriptions of your visuals. Think about your business, and use keywords that describe the image, but are also research-proven to drive targeted traffic.

If you aren't sure what keywords to use, I have a great SEO guide which can be accessed via www.thinkdigitalfirst.com

2. Create Collaboration Boards

Whilst it's great to have your own Pinterest boards that other people can look at, you should also look at creating boards where you audience can collaborate with you. The more you do this, the more likely YOU are to be invited into other boards as a collaborator.

3. Buyable Pins

Did you know that you can buy a product INSIDE Pinterest, without having to leave the platform? Pinterest's Buyable Pins is a great way to showcase your products. There is now a search section inside Pinterest where you can find ONLY pins that are 'buyable', and you should be utilising this as a part of your Pinterest for business strategy.

4. Promoted Pins

How much do you know about Promoted Pins? These are a way to organically promote your pins to your audience. This is similar to boosting a post inside Facebook, and can have three goals; awareness, engagement and traffic.

I have been using Pinterest ads for quite some time, and find them effective in reaching my audience members who actively engage inside Pinterest.

5. Consistency

For Pinterest to give you the results that you are looking for, you need to be consistent. This means that you must post every day, not just once a week. Don't only add your own pins, re-pin as well.

6. Make Your Website Mobile-Friendly

If you are looking to drive traffic to your website from Pinterest, you need to get mobile-friendly. Studies suggest that 75% of Pinterest usage takes place on a smartphone, so if you want to convert your Pinterest views into website views, make sure you are mobile-friendly.

7. Image Backlinking

A great strategy I use for Pinterest is to re-pin an image, and then change the description and URL behind it so that it redirects back to my website.

INSTAGRAM

It blows my mind to look at the list of social networks I talk about in this chapter and know that Instagram is one of the newest networks to hit the market. Current statistics show that 51% of Instagram users access the platform daily, and 35% say they look at the platform several times per day.

Since the first edition of this book, I would say that Instagram has seen the most change. We've seen new branding, as well as the introduction of a slideshow feature, Instagram Stories, new advertising options, updated analytical tools and a new integrated tool called Boomerang. Let's take a closer look at these changes.

Branding

In May 2016, Instagram completely changed their branding, redefining themselves as more forward-thinking. Instagram said:

"Our new logo is inspired by the previous app icon, the new one represents a simpler camera and the rainbow lives on in gradient form. We've made improvements to how the Instagram app looks on the inside as well. The simpler design puts more focus on

your photos and videos without changing how you navigate the app. The Instagram community has evolved over the past five years from a place to share filtered photos to so much more - a global community of interests sharing more than 80 million photos and videos every day. Our updated look reflects how vibrant and diverse your storytelling has become."

Instagram Slideshow

In 2017, Instagram introduced their Slideshow feature. Whilst a very simple addition, it has increased the platform's popularity, especially when it comes to small businesses marketing online.

This new feature allows you to upload 10 photos/videos in one single post. The photos/videos could be a behind-the-scenes look at your working week, it could be the latest product/service launch or even an event you are attending - the options are endless with the slideshow feature.

How To Use Instagram's New Slideshow Feature

When you go to add a new picture/video to your feed, follow these steps.

1. Click on the 'select multiple' option on the right hand side of the image.
2. Highlight the 10 (or fewer) images/videos you want to share on your profile
3. Click 'next'
4. Add a filter to your first photo then scroll through all your other slideshow photos
5. Click 'next'
6. Add content and hashtags as you would usually and upload your slideshow to Instagram!

Instagram Stories

Instagram stories allows you to share moments throughout your day, whether it be photos or videos that appear in a slideshow format for all of your followers to see, and experience, for up to 24 hours. Whilst some may say that Instagram Stories is just a mirror of the already existing, and successful Snapchat (which I talk about later on in this chapter), I would have to disagree. This feature may allow you to do exactly the same thing as Snapchat but don't forget the importance of Instagram as an engagement network as a whole.

How To Use Instagram Stories

Once inside your Instagram app, you will be able to see, at the top of your newsfeed profile pictures inside a circle of those who have created an Instagram Story. See visual below.

Here is the step by step process to creating your own story.
1. Click on the plus button which is found at the top left-hand side of your home screen.
2. Tap on the circle button at the bottom of your screen to take a photo, or hold to take a video.
3. Once you're happy you can edit the photo or video by adding text, drawings or by using the pen feature.
4. Click 'done' to save your story.
5. Click the check mark once you're happy and ready to share on Instagram!

Advertising
Because Facebook owns Instagram, you can access all of Instagram's advertising options inside Facebook.

When I run ads through Social Media, I now set my ads up inside Facebook, and can also manage Instagram's ads at the same time.

Instagram have four different advertising options:

Photo adverts
For Instagram's photo ads, use a square or landscape format visual to tell your story.

Video Adverts
I've been testing Instagram's video adverts over the last six months and have found them to be extremely successful. If you're going to use this option, make sure that you keep your video to under 60 seconds.

Carousel Adverts
If you want to use more than one image or video, take a look at the carousel advert option.

Stories Adverts
A new option from Instagram is the ability to use their Stories feature as a paid advertisement option for connecting with over 200 million people using stories daily.

Analytics
Instagram has offered users an inside look at their brand profiles with a 'contact' button, allowing users to directly email a business, or get directions to their store.

We have also seen the introduction of new analytics options – this includes the above, as well as a host of new insights and tools to give businesses the data they need to improve their Instagram marketing.

Instagram analytics will appear on the profile page section of an Instagram profile in the top bar next to the settings option.

Once inside analytics, you will see your Instagram insights. You'll be able to see all information regarding where your followers are geographically and what times your audience are on Instagram.

Knowing this will allow you to better organise your Instagram marketing, reaching your audience at the optimum time.

You will also have access to analytics that provide a gender and age breakdown of your audience, as well as data on how many impressions each of your posts generates.

Boomerang

Boomerang was created by Instagram as a way to make small, mini videos that loop back and forth in a more visually engaging way. Boomerang will take a burst of 10 photos in a matter of seconds, and turn them into a mini video. You can share this directly to Facebook and Instagram right from the app.

Layout

Instagram have made their image creation even more exciting for users by introducing their feature called Layout. With this new feature, you can create one-of-a-kind layouts and use your photos to create one main image that can be shared with your audience. You can add up to nine photos, tag people in the pictures, add text, and add a link.

YOUTUBE

When YouTube first hit the internet, I never realised that video would be so important. But Google did, which is why it brought YouTube. We, as consumers and businesses, are going to be creating more and more video content as a way of connecting with our audience online. It's going to be our main form of communication, and YouTube is a great place to share our video content.

12 years ago, the first video called 'me at the zoo' was uploaded by co-founder Jawed Karim and this started a trend of documenting our lives, and our businesses, via video.

Six out of 10 people prefer online video platforms to live TV. This is important because when it comes to spending money on advertising, you need to look at ways you can do this through video platforms rather than TV advertisement.

YouTube is here, and it's here to stay. Here are my top five tips to help you utilise YouTube for your business.

1. Create, Share And Collaborate On Playlists
Just like Spotify and iTunes, you can create video playlists and collaborate with other users. If you're going to create playlists of your videos, categorise them into different sections so that a potential customer can watch a selection of videos on a specific subject.

2. Add Text To Your Videos
I have realised that adding text to my videos before uploading them to YouTube has increased my click-through rate by 50%. I share with you a great tool in Chapter 5 that is free of charge, and will help you add text, transitions, music and images to your videos.

3. Custom YouTube URL
To make it easier for your audience to find you on YouTube, create your own custom URL that matches your branding. Make sure you're happy with your custom URL because once you've chosen it, you can't change it.

4. Add Clickable Links To Your Videos
Inside YouTube, there is a feature called Annotations which allows you to add call-to-action buttons to approved websites, as well as adding a subscribe button, and suggesting another video for them to watch.

5. Use Polls
When you're editing your video, there's a feature called 'Cards' where you can add a card to your video. This could be a link to another video, or a poll. If you're asking a question in your video or discussing a specific topic, consider adding a poll to get your audience engaged.

YouTube Community
With YouTube being the world's second largest search engine, and third most visited site after Google and Facebook, it was only a matter of time before YouTube followed in the footsteps of Google and created it's own social network.

The social network will allow you, as a video creator on YouTube, to better engage with your YouTube viewers using GIF's, text, images and more. This, in turn will help you to connect on a more personal level with your audience. This is shown as a tab on your channel called 'Community'.

GOOGLE+

Although Google+ is still a prominent network, it's one that's easily forgotten. Offering images, videos, content, communities and much more, it stands side-by-side with some of the longer running networks which offer the same type of features.

As a small business, what do you want to get from using Google+?

In my opinion, you need to include it in your overall marketing mix, from a branding and SEO perspective. Yes, it's possible to build a community if you already have a large client base and database who use Google+.

The newly named Google Business offers business owners a suite of tools to help build the presence of your online brand, from places, to events, photos to video, live streaming via hangouts. In Chapter 6, I will share with you a strategy which got me on the front page of Google, using my Google+ account based on targeted, and niche keywords.

SNAPCHAT

Snapchat was launched in 2011, and in just two years, had five million daily users. Fast forward a few years and Snapchat now has 100 million daily active users.

Snapchat is a new addition to this chapter, and one of the newest, and most popular social networks to date. With 54% of Snapchat users logging into their account every day and 87% of users using the app at least twice a week, you could be missing out on traffic and potential sales.

If you are looking to use Snapchat, here are some of the important features you need to know about.

Snap

This is a picture or video you upload to the app and share with the people who follow you. A snap can last up to 10 seconds.

Stories

When you have uploaded a number of snaps, you can create a story so that people can watch/look at a video/picture in a sequence.

Filters
Take one of your snaps, and add an overlay, just like you would inside Instagram. The available filters change on a regular basis depending on where you are based, holidays and the time of day.

Snap Lenses
Add animated special effects to your photos. You use a snap lens whilst you are taking a snap, rather than adding this after you have completed your snap.

Geofilter
Turn on your location inside SnapChat to access filters based on your location. You can also create your own filter for as little as $5 which can be a great way to increase brand awareness.

Snapcode
This is your unique QR code. When someone scans this, it will automatically add you to their friend list.

Chat
This is Snapchat's version of Instant Messenger. Once a message has been viewed, it disappears, so make sure you take a screenshot of this chat if you want to save it.

Memories
Because Snapchat is real time, a snap only lasts for 24 hours, so if you want to save them, it will be through using a camera roll feature called Memories. These can be public or private.

Here is what you should consider when using Snapchat.

Make it engaging
Add filters and overlays to your snap so that it keeps your audience engaged.

Captions
Add text to your Snap by using the captions feature marked as the 'T' icon.

Doodle
This is Snapchat's drawing tool where you can write text, or draw an image.

Timing
You can choose how long you want your snap to last for.

Whatever social network you decide is right for your personality, your business or where your target audience hang out, always make sure you put your best foot forward and Think #Digital First. Give the user an experience they will fall in love with, over and over again, and remember to always add your social icons in your various online profiles, including your website. Also, have your Social Media links on your printed literature from business cards and leaflets to banners at all public events and tradeshows.

DIGITAL MARKETING

When looking to launch a new product/service an old mentor of mine always used to say 'intelligence high, emotions low'. In other words, if the product is ready to be marketed, and you are emotionally excited about launching it, the intelligent thing to do is wait until you can generate such a buzz around the product/service - ultimately resulting in far better Key Performance Indicators (whatever KPIs are important to you).

Digital Marketing can be defined as:

> *"...an umbrella term for the marketing of products or services using digital technologies, mainly on the internet, but also including mobile phones, display advertising, and any other digital medium."*

Why Is Digital Marketing So Important?

Staying Laser-Focused On Your Target Audience

Your Digital Marketing strategy should be built around your target audience. They are what will make or break your business and to do this, you must do your research on them. Staying laser-focused on my audience has allowed me to engage with them on multiple platforms, at different touchpoints.

"NOT EVERYONE
is your
TARGET CUSTOMER "

It Is The Framework To Your Overall Marketing Plan
I think of Digital Marketing as the blueprint to my overall marketing strategy which I can build on, and integrate with my other marketing strategies. Without a Digital Marketing plan, you do not have a marketing plan for success.

Conveying Your Brand's Story
Digital Marketing is a huge part of sharing your brand's story with your target audience online. People buy from people, and the storytelling aspect part of your strategy is crucial to online success. I've realised that my story is something my audience connects with, which I why I re-wrote the introduction to this book, to make sure that my 'story' was up-to-date.

Digital Marketing Levels The Playing Field
As a small business, Digital Marketing is so important if you want to compete with companies that are more well known or bigger than you are. You have the exact same Digital Marketing resources as every other business, so use them as a way to connect with your audience on a more personal level.

It Gets Results
The bottom line is that Digital Marketing DOES get results and that's why it's so important that you understand exactly how to use it to your advantage.

COMPETITIONS
Running a Social Media contest has so many advantages, but you need to know exactly how-to run and optimise them.

Why You Should Run A Social Media Contest
For your business to be a success online, you need to generate leads which turn into sales. One of the most effective ways to do this is through a Social Media competition or contest. I had a client just last year generate 2,700 leads and thousands of pounds in sales just from spending £100 running a Social Media competition over the course of five days. They can be very successful if you know how to run one.

Here are five things to consider when running a Social Media Contest.

1. Choose ONE Social Network
You should just choose the social network which you are most engaged on, and run the competition using that network. Most businesses choose to run a competition on Facebook using an approved third party app because this is where success can be easily measured.

2. Choose Your Third Party App
If you try to run a competition on Facebook without using a verified third party app, they will close your Facebook Page down for good. Take a look at Chapter 5 for some great tools to use.

3. Make It Easy To Enter
I see so many businesses setting 'guidelines' to enter their competition, which include giving their name, email address, telephone number, address, age, gender as well as having to share the contest with their friends, and following on the particular social network. This is a turn off. Keep it simple and easy for your audience to enter. Just ask for basic information like name and email address.

4. Have Rules In Place
You will always come across rule breakers online and you need to make sure you are clear with your rules and regulations to enter the contest. Keep these as simple as entering, but do make sure your audience are abiding by your rules.

5. Logistics
There are a few things you need to consider before starting your Social Media Contest. How long are you going to run the competition for? What is the prize? How are you going to choose the winner? How are you going to announce them?

Consider the above questions and make sure they are answered before creating your Social Media contest.

How To Tips For Engaging On Each Social Network
Depending on the network you choose, your approach should be different. Whilst I'm not going to take you through the specific how-to for each social network, I will share with you great tips for executing your Social Media contest on your desired network.

Facebook
If you are running a Facebook competition, consider advertising it on Facebook to make sure your audience are seeing the contest. Promoted Posts will help increase visibility whilst also promoting your contest to your target audience. This will generate more engagement, leads and entries for your business.

If your contest is based on someone submitting a photo or video, make sure you share the entries with your audience. This will give your audience an idea of what it looks like to enter, and encourage them to follow suit.

Twitter
When it comes to running a contest on Twitter, there are certain hashtags you should be using to reach a larger audience. Consider using both #Contest and

#Sweepstakes in your tweets as people will be searching to enter a contest with a prize they want to win.

You should also be tracking engagement throughout the duration of your contest. You can do this using one of the tools I mention in Chapter 5. Measure your mentions, retweets, favourites and engagement to see whether Twitter is the best platform for you to run a contest.

Instagram
Instagram is the social network for hashtags and you must adopt this approach when running a contest. Encourage users to use hashtags to enter, as well as engage with you as a brand. This will also make it easier to track progress.

You should also make sure your contests are topical, and relevant to the time of year. There is no point running a competition based on a winter scarf or jacket in the middle of summer.

Pinterest
Whilst Pinterest may not be your chosen social network to run a contest, you can use it as a way to increase your following on the social network. If getting followers is your end goal. get entrants to 'follow' you as a part of a condition to enter. You should also create a new Pinterest board if submitting a video or photo is a part of how people enter.

EMAIL MARKETING
If you decide to run a competition and ask for a name and email address; this is what is classed as a lead magnet. In other words, you are attracting your prospects by giving something away in return for capturing their name and email address. This is the starting process that enables you to build an email strategy around your contacts. Generating a new lead is the best way to build your email database. However, you should never buy lists unless they have been 100% qualified. Delivering highly relevant content is a strategic goal, which 67% of marketers say their business wants to achieve through email marketing.

Here are five things to consider for your email marketing.

1. Make email marketing a part of your customer acquisition journey
2. Use mobile optimisation
3. Use personalised templates
4. Give away great content and value
5. Know what you are going to share

Email marketing can be one of the most powerful tools for getting more sales for your small business. The biggest problem is that most small businesses don't understand how powerful it can be to personalise emails. Without the touch of personalisation, you could be missing out on a lot of engagement and new or repeat customers.

I have spent the last 10 years building an email database, which now has over 18,000 small businesses on it, and the one thing I have learnt is the importance of personalisation. It's all well and good my telling you this, but without factual evidence that this is the case, you might find it hard to believe.

" ALL MARKETING IS BETTER
— when you know —
WHO YOU'RE MARKETING TO "

Email provider Mailjet ran a study which revealed that UK internet users believe that personalised emails are the best way to get them to click on a link. As you can see below, 38.9% of 16-29 year olds said that personalisation was the second most important attribute that would make them click on an email. This percentage grows to 39.6% for 30-44 year olds, and to 42.9% for 45-59 year olds. Averaging out the below attributes, personalisation scores the highest with an average of 40.2%.

Here are my top three tips for achieving success through email marketing.

1. Personalise Emails Based On A Scoring System
Email automation in particular should run itself. But this can't happen unless you have a lead scoring system in place that defines certain behaviours or demographics. You can 'score' your leads however you like, but to be descriptive, use terms like 'prospect', 'warm', 'hot' and 'buying customer'.

Mapping this will allow you to have control over what each user will receive from you in terms of your email marketing. Base your model on the above, and the demographics (interests, gender, age, location) and their behaviour (attended a webinar, attended a talk).

2. Merge Tags
A merge tag inside an email marketing tool is an algorithm that takes a piece of personal data from a user inside a tool, giving you a nice way to personalise any email you send.

For example, I will use the first name merge tag in the subject line of an email. It will look something like 'Come and meet me at [TRADESHOW], Name!' Inserting the merge tag will take the first name of your contact, and slot it in whenever you use that piece of code.

For a merge tag to work, you are going to have to collect personal data when doing lead generation.

I will always ask for a first name and email address on any sign up forms I use, as I know this is what I need for my merge tag, and to personalise my email communication.

3. Integrate Your Email Tool With Your Lead Generation Tool
This is really important for me, as I have a lot of lead generation content. I offer different guides, strategies, templates and other types of content as a free download in exchange for a name and email address. To make this run smoothly, I integrate my email marketing tool (see Chapter 5 for some options) with my lead generation tool so that as soon as someone downloads one of my pieces of content, they enter an automation series.

"**HUMANS** *are not* **EXTINCT**,"

ʳing my email strategy, I've noticed a 10% increase in open rate, and
ᵃ in click through rate JUST by personalising the 'who is it from'
ᵤ subject line and of course, the content inside of the email.

As someone who has sent over 250,000 emails in a matter of months, I can
safely say that personalisation does generate more visitors, leads and sales for a
business whilst simultaneously building my credibility online.

BLOGGING
Some small businesses don't have the budget needed to run advertisements
and one of the only ways they can digitally market their business is by blogging.
There is some debate as to whether blogging is still as important as it used to be
and I can say for certain, it is.

In 2016, I was highly commended at the UK Blog Awards for the Marketing and
Communications category, as well as being a finalist for two categories in 2017.
I've spent the last 10 years blogging, and have found it to be one of the best
FREE traffic drivers to date.

I write an article on my Warren-Knight.com website every week and this is
posted on a Friday morning as per my online marketing strategy. On a Tuesday,
I post a blog to my ThinkDigitalFirst.com website and this has been one of the
best ways to validate myself as an influencer in my industry. If you struggle to
write or can't think of a title, don't worry, I'm going to share with you a tool to
help you with this in Chapter 5.

If you are new to blogging, here are 10 blogging ideas to inspire you to write
amazing content.

Guides
Regardless of your industry, you can always find a topic that will follow a guide-
like format. Beginner guides in particular are extremely popular.

Interviews
I have shared content where I've been interviewed, as well as content other
thought leaders have shared around interviews online. It's always good to read
something an influencer has said.

Trending Topics
Last year, one of my 'trending topic' articles went viral. It's had over 11,000 views,
1,400 likes and over 300 comments JUST on LinkedIn Pulse. Find out what's
currently trending in your industry, and tap into that 'buzz' when blogging.

Personal Stories

I have shifted the way I write content on my warren-knight.com website. I now come from a place of personal development and sharing my stories. Show your audience that you are a REAL person through blogging about your personal story.

Give Advice

Let your audience get to know you and your product. If you have an innovative product/service, give your audience advice on how they can best use it.

How-To's

This was a regular appearance for the 'needs' of my audience. This type of content is informative, easy to follow and step-by-step based. Articles of mine that fit these criteria include 'How To Find An Email Address In 60 Seconds', 'How To Write The Perfect Headline For A Blog', and 'How To Design A Digital Marketing Plan As A Small Business'.

Myth-Debunking

Regardless of your industry, there will be something everyone believes to be true, when in actual fact it couldn't be further from it. Position yourself as an influencer and use your experience to educate your audience.

Problem Solving

There is a pain you are solving with your product/service, so find out the biggest problems your audience face, and solve them through blogging.

Case Studies

Case studies are one of the best ways to give you the trust and authority to turn a potential customer into a paid customer. Get inspired by the content your competitors share about their customers, and do the same with yours.

Upcoming Industry Events

Do you want to keep your audience in-the-know? Write content on the latest events in your industry that you will also be attending.

List Articles

I know that my audience read my articles that are list based, e.g. '5 Ways To Nurture And Win New Customers', and '7 Tips To Writing Perfect Content'. Make sure your list has sharable content, and the longer your list is the less written content you need for each 'number'.

GUEST-BLOGGING

As well as blogging, you also need to consider guest-blogging, and how you can reach out to industry experts and share your content to their audience. I wrote an article for Social Media Examiner and it has received over 6,500 shares. I have had various thought leaders (including a CEO of one of the tools I talk about in this book) reach out to me, and give me a lifetime pro account completely free of charge.

The most powerful thing about being a guest contributor on such an influential website is that when someone shares it, I then get tagged in the post. Whilst the link someone shares will send them to the article, it has my biography at the bottom with links back to my website which has already proved extremely powerful for me, and I've been contacted by various industry influencers with potential collaboration opportunities.

Guest-blogging is a key part of your strategy online, especially when it comes to link building. One of the main reasons why a company will ask for exclusive content is so they don't have to compete with you over traffic. Basically, they don't want to be out-ranked and in essence; neither do you.

CONTENT MARKETING

I have always talked about the importance of having a website that is mobile-friendly, as more and more consumers read content using their smartphones to find out more about a product/service.

Content Marketing is such an important part of promoting your business online. 76% of businesses said that they would produce more content throughout 2016, and this will likely rise moving through 2017.

What Is Content Marketing?

Content Marketing can be defined as:

> "...a strategic marketing approach focused on creating and distributing valuable, relevant, and consistent content to attract and retain a clearly-defined audience and, ultimately, to drive profitable customer action."

I am going to break Content Marketing down into four different areas; written, visual, audio and video. Here are some unique ways you can use content marketing to share your business with your target audience based on the four core areas

1. Written
There are so many great ways you can connect with your audience through written content marketing. Here are some of my favourite ways that I connect with my audience.

Incentives
Incentives are a great way to market your business to your audience. Giving your customers an incentive to purchase from you e.g. "if you make this purchase in the next 24 hours, you get a 25% discount."

Contests/Giveaways
Contests/giveaways are one of the best ways to increase brand awareness, and is great for lead generation. Offer something for free and, in return, ask for a name and email address. Utilise Social Media to visually display your contest. Don't forget to encourage people to share your content online!

Email Marketing
Email marketing is a huge part of my Digital Marketing strategy. When I'm running a special offer on a product/service of mine, I always display this is in a visually engaging way and find that conversion is a lot higher when I do this. I will talk about this more later on..

Testimonials
Testimonials are a great way to build trust and give you the authority you need online. Take your testimonial one step further, and use video testimonials.

"IMAGES INCREASE BRAND AWARENESS

by

150%"

2. Visuals

Written content is one way to connect, but what about visuals? Here are some of my favourite visual types of content.

Infographics

I absolutely love infographics. They are a great way to share data (that otherwise might be boring to read) in an effective way. Spending some of your time creating an infographic will give you something to share online that your community will appreciate and share with their friends.

Quotes

Share quotes that are relevant to your audience in a visual way. Use Canva to create your visual quote, and share it on Social Media. Quotes are buzz-worthy pieces of information and tend to receive a lot of shares and retweets.

Slideshare Presentation

I absolutely love SlideShare and find it a great tool to use when I've delivered a new presentation at an event and can give my attendees the link to look at it again. I have had tens of thousands of views of my presentations and it's completely free to use.

3. Audio

When it comes to audio content marketing, the main form of communication is podcasts.

I find podcasts to be an amazing way to increase brand awareness. I have been a guest on a number of them, and try and make sure I'm booked for at least one podcast a month as they are a great way to talk about one specific subject, or to promote a new product/service.

Take a look at the podcasts in your industry, and reach out to them to become a guest. This year in particular has been great for me regarding podcasts, and I will continue to be a guest on them for the foreseeable future.

4. Video
Video content marketing is something I have briefly covered earlier on in this chapter. Live-streaming is a great form of video content, as is just a simple video. Use one of the video editing tools in Chapter 5 to create a professional video that you can share across multiple social networks.

Before we move on to repurposing content, I do want to share with you my top two tips around content marketing.

1. Tap Into Emotions
People buy from people. A purchasing decision is made based on an emotional feeling. Use visual content to build trust, confidence and to tap into the emotions of your target audience.

2. Humanise Your Brand
Give your online community an insight into your brand and the people behind it. Share images and videos of the day-to-day workings of your business. This will help your community understand your business better, and connect with it on a deeper level.

REPURPOSING CONTENT
All these ways to content market don't need to be used just once. You can repurpose your content. Creating an infographic once will allow you to share via all your social channels, email marketing and even on your blog. One piece of content can flow out to multiple sources.

A study conducted by Orbit Media Studios suggested that a blog post will take anywhere from one hour to more than six hours to complete. For me, a blog will take around two hours from start to publish.

Knowing this tells me that this is a huge investment of time, and it doesn't stop there. I then take this piece of content and share it across my social networks, as well as posting it on various other sites including LinkedIn Pulse, Business2Community and Medium.

You need to be aware of the 'rules' around repurposing content. Duplicated content can be defined as 'exact text that has been copied from one page, and pasted to a different page with no changes made'.

The biggest problem here is whether Google will penalise me for duplicating content. With the constant changes in Google's algorithm, the answer to this question changes based on how Google works.

I reached out to a friend and industry expert called Alasdair Inglis. Alasdair is Managing Director of We Are Grow, who focus on transforming marketing strategies and turning them into a profitable plan for business marketing online. Part of Alasdair's expertise includes SEO, and I want to share with you some of his words, to help you better repurpose your content, without being penalised for doing this.

Should You Use The Same Content On Your Web Pages Elsewhere?

Definitely do not duplicate this kind of content. If you are selling a product or service online and have spent the time and effort to rank for keywords around this product or service, duplicating this content will work against you.

Will Google Penalise You For Duplicating Content Across Other Sites?

Technically, yes; however it's a bit more complicated. By syndicating your content, particularly on the likes of LinkedIn Pulse and Medium, you are indeed reaching a whole new community of potential customers, but you do need to be aware that because LinkedIn Pulse and Medium are heavy-weight sites, they will likely outrank you, meaning the traffic to your website drops because it is being directed to the post on LinkedIn Pulse and Medium.

You do, however, get traffic you would not have otherwise have got from the likes of LinkedIn Pulse and Medium, so it is a trade-off.

1. Post The Content On Your Website First

You want to eliminate the potential of having to compete for traffic, so make sure the article you are thinking of duplicating actually sits on your website first.

2. Only Repurpose 50% Of Your Content

I say this because the importance of getting website traffic that converts is more important than maybe getting 10-50 views on the post elsewhere. Keep some of your content exclusive to your website, and only duplicate 50% of your blog content.

3. Wait One Month Until You Syndicate

If you are going to re-publish content elsewhere, give Google time to rank the post on your website before you share it on another website.

4. Keep An Eye On Website Traffic

Whilst I am saying re-purpose only 50% of your content, analyse this on a regular basis to see whether you are having a large drop in website traffic, as this may be the reason why. Google, being the wonderful beast that it is, is constantly changing the way its ranking algorithm works, and you will always want to be on top of this.

Once you have your content ready to market, you need to amplify it. Chapter 5 is about tools to help your business grow, and when it comes to amplification there are some great tools you can use to help you save time.

GOOGLE ADVERTS

If you decide that you want to spend money on native advertising, you can do so through PPC, which means you will pay for every designated click you receive to your website. I have spoken about all of the advertising options inside each social network, but now I want to talk about advertising on Google.

Google is always introducing new features, and I want to make sure you are aware of these changes, and how they impact your business.

New User Interface

Google has made a new user-interface change on their AdWords platform. What used to be clunky is now sleek and user intuitive. Whilst you may not be seeing this new interface yet, you will do in the next few months.

Life Event Targeting

As a business, you will have seasonal times of the year where certain holidays are more profitable than others. For example, if you sell a gift-type product, you will find an increase in website visits around wedding season, and around Christmas. Using this new AdWords feature means that you can advertise to people when they are most likely to buy a product/service from you.

In-Market Audience

The in-market audience feature will identify those who are nearing the end of their buying cycle, and are ready to purchase a product/service based on their searching and navigational history. Google can now identify these prospects, and target your ads to them.

Google Surveys 360

What if you could create a survey, send it to a sample audience and generate results? This is a great new addition, and one which makes A/B testing that much easier. Use this to get feedback on WHY someone clicked on your ad to give you a better understanding around what's working, and what isn't.

Accelerated Mobile Page Ads

According to Google, every additional second of landing page load time represents a 20% dip in conversion rate, which is why Google's AMP (accelerated mobile page) ads are worth your time. Use this tool to improve your page speed and send search traffic to your AMP through display ads.

Google Optimise

Google Optimise now integrates with AdWords, meaning you have a quicker and easier way to test landing pages. Landing pages are great for lead magnets, and this is how I use them. Think about how you can create landing pages that connect with your audience, and then test them through Google Optimise.

Landing Page Reporting

Understanding how your landing pages are performing is one step, but taking it further and actually generating a report that can be analysed is very powerful, and that's what Google Adwords will now let you do.

Google Assist

Voice payments are on the rise, and Google has revolutionised this and bought it to the market. How great could it be if your customer could pay for your product/service with just their voice?

That's what's new to Google Adwords, so take a look at the interface, and measure your successes and failures using the above tools.

BING

Google isn't the only search engine. Microsoft's Bing controls more than 20% of the world's search engines, mainly because countries such as China have banned the use of Google. You might decide you want to focus more time optimising your site for Bing and the good news is that its algorithm is similar to Google's in many ways. These have a large number of high-quality backlinks, and they also optimise URLs and domain names for keywords. However, there are some things you need to consider when optimising your website for Bing.

Bing favours older websites with more official domain names, for example .edu or .gov. Bing also knows how to index flash media (unlike Google) and has a stronger attachment to showing small business results rather than bigger businesses. Google and YouTube are the two biggest search engines in the world, and in my opinion Bing's popularity isn't substantial enough to focus a lot of time and effort on.

PUBLIC RELATIONS

Public Relations (PR) is the management of information being shared between a person and an organisation as a way to boost the profile of an individual or business. If you are looking to launch your business and want extra exposure for your product or service, the best way to reach those who are influential and might write about your business is through PR. If you don't know how to write a press release, here are some pointers to help you.

- Keep the headline of the Press Release relevant, clear and to the point.
- Use the keywords within your business to help you with this.
- Use a larger font for your headline because it is the first thing people read.
- Capture the feel of the press release in the first sentence of your main body text.
- Have the date and the city your company is based in, in the body text.
- Keep it simple to read and easy to understand. Avoid using long sentences as well as fancy language.
- Sum up the press release in the first paragraph, and the rest of the text should elaborate on this.
- Use the five W's (Who, What, When, Where and Why) to write your press release. Make sure you have information on each W in your document.
- Provide information links to support your press release.
- Include information about your company and contact details at the end of the press release, for the people who want to find out more.

If you know from Chapter 3 that writing isn't a strength of yours and your time is better spent elsewhere, you can hire someone to do this for you.

ENTERING AWARDS

Over the last three years, I have won six awards, and been a finalist in three others. I have been named a top-100 global influencer, a top-three digital influencer, 15th most influential marketer, top-10 business advisor and top-10 business coach, as well as Marketing Book of the Year finalist, and UK Blog Awards finalist to name a few.

Entering local, industry and business awards is a great way to market your business, build your profile in your industry, get accreditations and have something to talk about via a press release and across Social Media.

In one of my start-up technology companies we won many awards and were highly recommended in others, and this quickly built a name for our business in our industry, simply by focusing on writing a great story and spending a few hundred pounds on entering the awards.

I have had the pleasure of being a judge at various Digital Marketing awards, and because of this I wanted to share with you a few helpful tips. There are some very simple questions that need answering, however, the answers are not as easy as they seem. Firstly, which awards should you enter?

Never wait until an organisation approaches you to enter their awards procedure. Create a plan, know which awards you are going to enter before they accept entrants and be prepared for the difficult questions. Here are some things to ask yourself before entering:

- How much of your marketing budget have you allocated to entering awards?
- What do you want the award to say about your business?
- Are you focusing on local (regional), national or international awards?
- When are you going to be ready to tell your story?
- Are you ready with PR and marketing once you've won?

It sounds great to enter every single award in your industry in the hope that you get shortlisted for at least half, but think about the cost. Entries are usually priced from £50-£750 and that doesn't include the night of the awards, which will most likely cost from £99-£500 for just one seat.

To be fully prepared to enter an award, have a planning session with the people around you. Know your story, build up a file of case studies and have short but intelligent answers to potential questions. Winning an award is not easy, and it usually depends on how well you have presented your business in a written or verbal presentation.

Awards are not just based on a written entry. There is usually a second stage which is a presentation of some form to a panel of judges with a Q and A. This is a lot more challenging than a written entry, so make sure you know which awards require this from you, so you're as prepared as possible.

AFFILIATE MARKETING
Affiliate marketing is, in essence a sales strategy. An individual will share links to your products and receive a commission when they get a sale. This is otherwise known as Performance Marketing. According to AM Navigator, developed affiliate programs account for generating 15% to 30% of all advertisers online sales. This has changed because of the increase in businesses using Social Media advertising. However, Affiliate Marketing should not be ignored.

To make your Affiliate Marketing a success, you need to be able to communicate. This needs to be regular, especially with key affiliates and clear, concise and straight to the point. This process teamed with planning, clear commercials, great product feeds and banners along with incentives and promotions are what will make your Affiliate Marketing a success.

To have a totally socially-savvy business, where you've thought about every sales and marketing opportunity utilising everything I have mentioned in this chapter, takes time. It takes weeks of preparation, implementation and analysing the results to make sure you are always increasing your brand awareness, lead generation and ultimately sales. Take baby steps and each day focus on achieving a small goal, which always moves the business forward.

PARTNERSHIPS

This is one of the only three ways to generate new business in your company and has always been a massive focus of mine in every business I've started and grown, providing access to new prospects and customers that bring in new business on a monthly basis.

Some people like to call this as JV (Joint ventures) or Affiliates which I've touched on above. For me, building a relationship with a 'channel partner' who has a long-term goal is a win-win scenario. Partnerships do not always mean cash is exchanged; it can also be an exchange of knowledge.

Let me explain in more detail and break it down into four simple steps.

Step One: Determine A Channel Partner Strategy
When it comes to creating a channel partner strategy, there are three different options you can look at for working with other companies.

Sell Through Your Partner
If you work with retailers who sell your products for you, then you already have a 'partnership' in place.

Your Partner Sells Through You
The same as the above, but vice versa e.g. a business that offers your product/ service as a way to expand what they are offering as a business.

Your Partner Sells For You
This could be someone who works as your advertiser or promoter and will promote your product/service, and make the sale for you.

Once you know which route to go down, we can move onto step two. As someone who works with various different partners, I sell through my partners, and my partners also sell for me.

Step Two: Identify Relevant Partners

When you are looking to build a partnership, there are certain questions you need to ask yourself:

- What market do you want to reach?
- Does your partner offer the same products/services as you do?
- Do they complement your product/service?
- Do they have the database to reach a large number of your target audience?
- Are you solving a need for their database?
- How likely are your partner's customers to purchase?

Once you have asked yourself these questions, score each of your potential partners. Mark those who meet at least 80% of your criteria as VIPs, and mark those who do not score so well as secondary targets.

Step Three: Develop A Plan

Now that you've decided on the type of partnership you want, and identified the partners you want to work with, you need to develop a plan that allows you to connect with them through a value proposition.

Start with the easier partners to speak with, talk about ways in which you can help their audience, and bring them on board before approaching the VIPs. The more you are seen to work successfully with partners, the more likely the VIPs are to work with you.

Step Four: Drive Business Growth And Trust

Continue to work with your partners to boost sales, and build trust within your industry. The more you work with partners on a mutually-beneficial agreement, the more you will build trust and growth as a business.

BRAND ADVOCATE

Brands that generate the most brand awareness online are those that connect with their customers, promoting brand advocacy at every stage of the customer acquisition journey.

What Does A Brand Advocate Mean?

A brand advocate is a customer who speaks favourably about a product/service through word of mouth, or other marketing avenues.

A brand advocate may be:

- A famous face or VIP who relays a positive image e.g. a blogger or industry expert
- A person who has a strong knowledge about a brand e.g. a friend

or customer
- A person who will advertise your brand for free, using their social connections.

A brand advocate will strongly believe in the product/service they are spreading the word about, and when you start working with these brand advocates, you need to have a plan in place for what you want to achieve.

When onboarding new advocates, communication is vital, and will make or break the success. Here are few things to think about:

- Follow users that follow you, and engage with the content they share
- Shout-out community members who contribute positively to your online discussions
- Don't skimp on likes and shares
- Reward the people who stand out in your community
- Send them swag or discounts
- Send them hand-written letters.

My final tip is to go all-in and get your staff, friends, family and customers to all post, share, like, and mention your business from day one. The louder the noise you make, the bigger reach you have.

INFLUENCER MARKETING

Did you know that 92% of consumers have made a purchase after reading about a product on their favourite blog? A further 65% are likely to make a purchase if someone they follow on Social Media recommends a product.

As the concept of influencer marketing is still relatively new, I decided to add this in the rewrite to share with you what influencer marketing is, and its importance.

What Is Influencer Marketing?

The idea is to have people who are influential online spread the message about your business for you. This type of marketing can be in the form of blogger reviews, Social Media posts, endorsements and various other forms of content.

We have seen how influential this can be, especially on YouTube. Influencers on YouTube are often sent new product releases and in exchange, they talk about it to their audience. In some cases, influencers use 'sponsored' content, which means that they are being paid to talk about a product/service.

81% of marketers who have executed influencer marketing campaigns agree that it is an effective form of communication.

"SOCIAL MEDIA
— *turns a* —
HANDSHAKE
INTO A HUG,,

Why You Should Use Influencer Marketing

When you decide to use influencers to spread the word about your product/ service, it can be extremely effective, and here are three reasons why.

1. Trust

This type of marketing relies heavily on trust. Someone else who has earned trust else over a long period of time, and who calls attention to your business, actually sells your products/services.

2. Reach A Larger Audience

The reason why most businesses will turn to Influencer Marketing is to reach their target audience in a more direct, and broader way (especially if the business doesn't have the same kind of reach). Having specific influencers for your niche audience means that you are targeting the right people, rather than relying on them seeing your message online.

3. Cost Effective

It may cost you to send some of your products out to influencers for them to review. This will be a small cost compared to what it would cost you to make the same the amount of sales using various other marketing efforts. Whilst you may find that paying for sponsored content will cost you more than you think, the influencer will guarantee that your product/service will be seen by a large number of your target audience and will give you a great return on investment.

Here are my top three tips when it comes to working with influencers online.

1. Have A Story To Tell

Influencers are more than just popular. They captivate their audience, and persuade them to buy a product/service. To make going down this route worthwhile, you need to have an engaging story to tell.

2. Set Expectations

If you're going to spend money with an influencer, set the expectations around what you want to achieve from the get go. Keep everything friendly, but explain that it is important that your expectations are matched. Ask for their media kit so that you can see their audience demographics in more depth.

3. Start Small

Reaching out to influencers with millions of followers may be costly, so consider reaching out first to those in your industry who have a slightly smaller audience to make sure that going down this route will be worth your time and money.

In Chapter 6, I'll be talking about your sales and marketing plan, where all of these actions can be planned out and executed with laser focus precision.

FIVE

TECHNOLOGY FOR BUSINESS SUCCESS

CHAPTER 5

Since launching my online training platform; ThinkDigitalFirst.com, I've been testing out a number of new tools which have helped me and my team not only to work collaboratively, but to stay focused on the tasks at hand.

The tools that I mention in this book are here to help you grow a business, whether that's locally, nationally or internationally.

Some of the tools mentioned in the original copy of Think #Digital First are no longer around, or have been outperformed by alternative tools taking the market by storm.

Part of growing a business online is understanding the importance of registering your domain name as early as possible. Regardless of whether you are ready to create a website, you can still leverage your domain name through:
1. Company-branded emails
2. Redirects to your Social Media pages and/or;
3. Splash/Landing pages

I'll share with you a selection of tools that will help you leverage your domain name, broken down into 6 different categories;

1. Research and Listening
2. Design
3. Marketing
4. Business
5. Search Engine Optimisation
6. Data

RESEARCH AND LISTENING

Growing your business and using online marketing as a way of achieving success is all about being able to research your competitors and customers. By listening to them talking about what pain they are in, your business can help solve that pain. Without listening to the needs of your customers, how will you know whether the product/service you want to launch online will actually solve their problem?

The following seven research and listening tools have helped me to create and find content to share with my audience, to listen in to the latest trends so that I can deliver relevant content, to analyse real-time searches across multiple social networks and to find online influencers in my industry.

Alltop

Built by the powerhouse that is Guy Kawasaki, Alltop has been around for close to 10 years. Whilst it may not be the most visually appealing tool I will share with you in this section of the book, its algorithm works. Just type in the subject you are looking to find relevant content for, and it will give you the five most recent pieces of content from specific, industry-leading content sites.

BuzzSumo

This tool was relatively new to the market when I originally wrote this book, so it hadn't had time to make enough of an impression for me to include it in my book; until now.

Founded in 2014 in Brighton, East Sussex; BuzzSumo is a UK-based tool that analyses what content performs best for any specific topic, or key competitor. You can use this tool to find the content that has been shared the most as well as what is currently trending in real-time, learn who the top influencers are for that subject, and monitor engagement inside Social Media.

BuzzSumo is being used by the likes of IBM, Expedia, BuzzFeed, Vimeo and TED, to name a few.

Feedly

Feedly has been on the market for close to 10 years, and since its launch has been one of my most used and loved researching tools. Feedly will give you the ability to find online content in your industry, and keep it in one central place.

The biggest reason Feedly is one of my favourite tools is because of how visual I am. Being able to click on a category, e.g. Social Media, will give me a breakdown of the latest articles from websites that I've added to that category. It will also show you how recently an article was posted, so that you know whether it is 'trend worthy' or slightly out of date.

Google Trends

When it comes to visualising the real-time trends worldwide, Google Trends is the tool to use. This is a new addition to the tools section of this book and one which I now use on a regular basis.

You can narrow down your search trends based on five different categories, including 'top stores' and also search based on specific locations. Because Google is the largest search engine in the world, Google Trends is able to pull in billions of conversations happening online to give you the best, and most accurate, results.

Medium

Medium is all about reading, writing and sharing stories that matter to your audience. It was founded by Twitter co-founder Evan Williams in 2012. It was initially developed as an evolved version of Twitter to share content longer than their 140-character maximum, but now it runs as a completely independent tool and is described as being "your daily news reimagined, straight from the people who are making and living it. Discover and follow your favourite writers and the stories that matter to you, every day."

Mention

Mention has been around since 2012, and is a great tool to use when looking for real-time searches across your social networks, and the internet in general.

This tool allows you to complete real-time monitoring, competitive analysis, find influencer insights and create automated reports. You can track everything that's important to growing your business online, as well as engage with your audience with a better understanding of what will build your brand awareness. Mention is used by the likes of Airbnb, Microsoft, Adobe and Deliveroo.

Tagboard

If there is one tool that I loved, and used religiously throughout 2016, it was Tagboard. Search a topic, or hashtag, and you will see the real-time results of that search term across all social networks. This is a great way to monitor mentions about your business, and also to give you inspiration for your next blog post.

DESIGN

2017 has been the year of visual and video marketing. 37% of marketers said visual marketing was the most important form of content for the business, second to only blogging.

It's true that people are only likely to remember 10% of the information that they hear three days later. Combine this with a relevant image, and their recall rate increases to 65% over the same time period.

With the tools the market is using evolving from images into GIFs, into video and now live streaming, there are various ways you can connect with your audience through visual marketing.

Animoto

Are you looking for a tool that will allow you to create professional looking videos using photos as a slideshow? Take a look at Animoto. Animoto became the first video sharing site to support consumers in 2007 and has been a go-to tool of mine to add music behind a video, and create slideshow videos.

Canva

Without a doubt, Canva is my favourite image creation tool, and I've been using it daily ever since it hit the market in 2012. It's an amazing and simple designing software with the capabilities of Photoshop but without the clunky software, or expensive price tag.

We are now in the era of visual marketing, and creating professional images should be at the top of your list. Create a free account on Canva, and have a play around. You will be surprised to find out how easy it is to create visuals that look like they are worth a million pounds.

iMovie / Windows Movie Maker

If you're looking for a video editing tool but don't want to spend hundreds of pounds on the likes of Final Cut Pro, take a look at iMovie Maker (for Mac users) and Windows Movie Maker (for Windows users).

The software is simple, easy to use, and provides a professional video for you to share online and across Social Media. You can add text, visuals, transitions, music and more.

PicMonkey

When Google decided to shut down Picnik in 2012, two of their engineers left the company and created PicMonkey. You can crop, rotate and add overlays to your photos as well as various other more advanced options. You can try PicMonkey for free, and upgrade to their paid platform for access to their more extensive feature list.

Piktochart

A new addition to this tool chapter is Piktochart. Piktochart is an easy-to-use infographic creator. Take your visual content to the next level without having to hire a professional designer to do the work for you. Piktochart have over 600 professionally designed templates for you to choose from, meaning there will always be something perfect for what you want.

Slideshare

Slideshare is different to the other visual tools I have talked about, because it is a network that allows you to post your presentations so that your community can view it at a later date. I use this tool to host my presentations, and webinar seminar slides to give people the chance to view them at a later date, should they wish to do so.

Snapseed

Snapseed has been one of my favourite smartphone app tools to add filters, text and other different effects. It was rated as one of the top 100 best Android Apps of 2015 by PC Magazine. The tool is completely free of charge for Android and Apple users alike.

Visme

Visme is a new addition to this extensive list of amazing design tools, and one which has impressed me especially over the last few months. Engage your audience with powerful visual stories using Visme. You can create professional looking presentations, infographics and other visual content in just a matter of minutes, and...Visme is completely free of charge.

MARKETING

There are thousands of tools on the market that will help you with the marketing of your business. Building your online presence is key, and there are tools you can use to help you do this.

Blog Idea Generator

How many times have you been stuck, unable to come up with an idea for your blog, and actually not written it because of this? I know when I first started writing content that I was always stuck for ideas, and found Blog Idea Generator to be a great tool to get me started.

This tool is one of HubSpot's selection of great algorithms to give you the inspiration to write content that your audience will love.

The tool works by giving you the option to input three different nouns and then generate blog titles based on those keywords. Their algorithm isn't perfect (as they say themselves), so use this tool as it should be used; as an idea generator.

A key part of taking your business online and growing a successful business is about amplification. How can you take your message, and share it online just once, and have this amplified across multiple platforms? Here are four tools to help you do just that.

ClickFunnels

For me, marketing funnels are so important to engage with my audience on a regular basis through an automated process. ClickFunnels allows you to automate all of your processes and build landing pages that will convert visitors into leads and then into sales. If you are overwhelmed by the idea of building a website and all of the different tools, consider ClickFunnels as a great option to build landing pages using done-for-you templates.

Hootsuite

Hootsuite has been my favourite Social Media scheduling tool for a number of years. You can integrate the likes of Facebook, Twitter, Google+ and LinkedIn and manage all of the messages you share across each network in a matter of seconds.

Hootsuite helps me save a lot of time, because you can schedule in advance. Now being a father means that my time is even more precious, so a tool like Hootsuite that helps me save time when it comes to Social Media is a big plus in my book.

Instapage

I have been using Instapage for the last two years, and have found it to be an amazing lead magnet. If you are looking for engaging, one-page landing pages to generate leads, Instapage is a great option. They have a number of different templates, and price plans to suit everyone's needs.

Schedugram

You may have noticed that I didn't say Instagram as a network you can schedule information to using Hootsuite, and that is because there isn't functionality there to let this happen. But I do have a tool that will allow you to schedule to Instagram and that's called Schedugram.

Schedugram is not a free tool, but if Instagram is the social network that has your target audience and that you find engagement is highest there, then Schedugram will be worth the cost, especially if you know you're going to get a ROI (return on investment).

The next two tools I want to share with you under the 'business growth' banner will help you craft content using inspiration from an 'idea generator' tool, and rank the title of your content to make sure it's relevant, specific and what your target audience wants from you..

CoSchedule Title Ranker

Have you ever sat down to write an article and stumbled at the first hurdle of trying to write the title?

CoSchedule has a great, free title-ranking score tool that will help you drive traffic, shares and search results around your content. The title is the first thing a visitor will see when looking at your content, so use this tool to make sure your title is connecting with your audience.

ViralWoot

Specifically for Pinterest, ViralWoot is a scheduling tool that also provides analytical information about your Pinterest account. You can also manage multiple Pinterest accounts, and look at setting up pin alerts. Viralwoot is used by 65,000 individuals and businesses and does give a great insight into your Pinterest analytics.

As a business, you should be looking at as many ways as possible to generate customer leads and drive campaign traffic. One of the best ways to do this is by running a competition. Below is the one and only tool I use to run any competition, and I have had great success using this tool.

Shortstack

Shortstack is a great, cost effective tool to use for running competitions. You are given hundreds of templates to choose from, or you can create your own competition from scratch. Shortstack integrates with Facebook, meaning that you can have a link inside your Facebook Business Page where your 'fans' can enter the competition.

There are many ways you can engage with your consumers. Here are five tools to help you converse in real time, increase conversions, run a meeting via a webinar and conduct a survey.

Gotowebinar

Gotowebinar is a piece of software which I've used for years, allowing me to run monthly webinars to more than 100 people. It comes with a 30-day free trial and allows you to customise and record your webinars, so your customers can watch it in their own time.

The biggest reason I use Gotowebinar is because of how robust the system is. I know I can trust Gotowebinar to deliver a quality webinar, whilst also giving me access to analytics of who attended, and who didn't.

ManyChat

Do you have a strong following on Facebook and want to connect with them on a more personal level? Take a look at messenger bot ManyChat as a way to reach your customers in their Facebook messenger inbox so that you can engage in a two-way conversation.

OptinMonster

OptinMonster has been one of the best leader generators for me throughout 2017. Whilst I am new to this tool, the tool is not new to me. OptinMonster is a powerful lead generation software that converts abandoning visitors into subscribers with dynamic marketing tools through pop-ups.

I have set up various pop-ups to appear on my websites at different moments. I have one which is set up to appear within 30 seconds of someone being on my website, and I also have a different pop-up which will show up with someone who is about to exit my site. I use my free resources to generate leads, as well as promote webinars.

PushCrew

PushCrew is another new tool to this chapter, and one which has allowed me to capture the interest of hundreds of people through push notifications. People can 'opt-in' to receive these notifications through my website, which means I can then share with them my latest blogs, webinars and products.

SurveyMonkey

If I'm going to run a survey to my audience, I will either use Google Forms, or SurveyMonkey. This tool will give you analytical results so that you can better plan your next product based on the feedback of your audience.

Just like Google Forms, SurveyMonkey is free.

Zoom

If you find that Gotowebinar doesn't work for you, or is out of your budget, take a look at Zoom as a great alternative. Zoom is an American-based company, and offers a wide range of video conferencing options as well as screen sharing, meeting and instant messaging.

Zopim (Zendesk)

Zopim is a free live chat software which allows you to engage with consumers in real-time using a messenger-like website plug-in. This is a much faster and more personal way to connect with your consumers who have queries in real-time.

You can set up automated responses so that if you're busy, and can't reply within 60 seconds, they will be told that you are going to attend to their question shortly.

Have you thought about the importance of Inbound Marketing? If so, take a look at the tool below as a great option to help you manage marketing automation.

Now we move onto Email Marketing, which is a key part of my marketing strategy and should be a part of yours too. Building a database of names and emails is what will help a business succeed online, but which tool are you using to engage and nurture your leads? I have four options for you below.

ActiveCampaign

I have recently switched from Mailchimp to ActiveCampaign and I have found that whilst Mailchimp is a great tool, it was missing a lot of functionality that I needed as the opportunity for growth increased.

ActiveCampaign is one of the best email marketing tools on the market. You can manage contacts with tags, and schedule automations based on this. Using ActiveCampaign has made it easier to manage every name and email address by tagging them every time they take an action.

Mailchimp

Mailchimp is the world's leading email marketing tool and offers great templates, analytics, autoresponder, list creation, and personalisation. It's completely free of charge (unless you have more than 2,000 contacts).

If you are a small business on a tight budget and want a simple platform, Mailchimp will be perfect for you.

BUSINESS

Business growth is something that I have specialised in for the last 10 years, and during this time I've come across some amazing tools that cover a variety of different business needs.

The first three I'll share with you will help you find experts to complete tasks where you need specific expertise, to save time and to delegate so that you can spend the time focusing on growing your business.

99Designs

If you are time short and have decided that you can't focus on the designing side of your business, use this tool to find someone to help you.

99designs works by creating a proposal, and giving the designers on 99designs a chance to pitch their design options. You may end up with over 100 potential designers who have submitted a visual that matches your brief. You choose your favourite design, and then pay for it. In essence, it's like working with hundreds of designers and only having to pay for one!

Fiverr

Do you struggle to create images, or content that connects with your audience? Hire someone for as little as $5 on Fiverr to do it for you. Fiverr is an online marketplace where you can have one-off jobs completed at a small cost.

There is one downfall with Fiverr; quality. Spend some time finding the right person to complete the job for you and always look at reviews. As you are paying a very small fee, you might find that some of what you get done is verging on mediocre so just be careful, and do your research before paying someone to complete a task for you.

Upwork

Whether you are looking for programmers, web developers, designers or writers, Upwork may be the tool for you. Hiring skilled professionals to complete tasks based on their expertise is essential. and for a fraction of the usual cost; Upwork will give you an extensive list of thousands of potential 'experts' to help you complete a task at hand.

The next four tools are what I use on a daily basis to collaborate with my team so that we are all on the same page, and can keep track of each other's progress when we have targets, goals and challenges we need to meet, and overcome.

Dropbox

Dropbox's initial release in 2007 paved the way for cloud storing applications, as it was one of the first of its kind to offer users a free place to store important pieces of content and files in a safe and secure environment that didn't require you to store anything on your laptop, computer or smartphone.

As a basic user on Dropbox you have access to 2GB of free data storage. Anything over this, and there will be a monthly cost, but for the security of your files, and freeing up space on your computers and smartphones, Dropbox is worth every penny.

Dropbox also allows you not only to create a multitude of folders, but to invite your team into these folders and see real-time updates and additional files being added/removed, making sure you and your team are as up-to-date as possible.

Google Drive

Google Drive has to be one of my most used day-to-day tools. I use Google Docs, Google Spreadsheets, Google Forms and Google Slides for various different actions. I use Google Docs to create word documents that my team and I can collaborate on in real-time, and the same for Google Spreadsheets.

I use Google Forms to create surveys which I send to my audience to get feedback on products and services that I deliver. I use Google Slides for my webinar and seminar presentations. I can invite my team members into any of the Google Drive files I create, and we can all work on the same file at the exact same time.

You will need a Google account to use Google Drive, but this is completely free of charge, and will come in handy when it comes to creating a YouTube channel, or Google+ account (both require a Google account to use the networks).

HighriseHQ

I first started using HighriseHQ back in 2011 and loved the tool. I then tried a few different other CRM tools, but have found myself back using HighriseHQ since the end of 2016.

My team and I use HighriseHQ to manage relationships between partners, brands and customers. We can track all email conversations with specific contacts as well as tag contacts, add notes and set date and time-specific tasks.

Highrise is a paid tool but worth every penny in my opinion. If you find that your follow-up strategies with clients and customers is somewhat lacking, or you aren't holding yourself accountable for keeping in touch with clients, take a look at HighriseHQ.

Trello

Trello is a great collaborating and task management tool. I use it by creating boards based on a specific focus, and creating cards with strategies on managing processes within my business.

We also have a 'daily tasks' board with checklists and time-based actions so that we are all on the same page when it comes to the most important tasks for that specific date. All of our projects can be tracked very easily, and best of all; Trello is completely free of charge.

When it comes to time management, which tools are you using to effectively manage your time on a day to day basis so that you are not being a busy fool, and are focusing on what's important to your business? Here are two of my favourite time management tools that help me cut corners on certain tasks.

Evernote

Evernote is the first time management tool I want to talk about. It allows you to keep all your work in one place and it integrates with your Gmail so you can save emails and never have to waste time trying to find an important email ever again.

Evernote also has a great mobile app that will sync with the desktop version of the tool so that you can be up-to-date on every device you use.

Question: Which website builder/eCommerce platform have you used to create your website/online store? If you are thinking about switching providers, or looking at building your first website, take a look at the below four options that are my 'go-to' website building tools.

Squarespace

Squarespace, created in 2014, is an all-in-one eCommerce solution to creating a professional multi-channel website.

Squarespace is probably the least well known platform out of the four I am going to share with you but they have a wide range of templates for creating a professional website. Regardless of whether you want a website or online store; Squarespace will have some amazing options for you to take advantage of.

Wix

Wix was developed in 2006 and is a cloud-based web development platform. It is known as being one of the easiest website creators with drag and drop functionality.

If you want something that is cost effective, and can be used by someone who is not very tech-savvy, take a look at Wix. It has hundreds of customisable templates, and provides a website building platform to over 100 million users.

WooCommerce

New to this list is WooCommerce. Whilst WooCommerce is not a website build per se, it is one of my most valuable website tools. WooCommerce is an open source eCommerce plugin for Wordpress created websites. This tool is very easy to install into your Wordpress website, and allows you to take payments almost instantly.

In May 2015 WooCommerce was acquired by Automattic; operator of Wordpress.com. If Wordpress believes in the ability of this tool, then so do I.

WordPress

In my opinion, WordPress is the best website builder on the market. My Warren-Knight.com website, and my ThinkDigitalFirst.com website have both been built inside WordPress. Since March 2016, WordPress has been reportedly powering 26.4% of the web. This continues to rise, and it is still the most used CMS, with 59.4% market share.

You have access to over 44,200 different plugins so you will never be left without a solution to your problem. I can't recommend WordPress as a website builder enough. It has an intuitive interface and with its endless selection of plugins, and design options, you will be able to create a professional looking website no matter what your budget.

Following on from Website building, I want to mention one particular company that I use to take all my payments, and have done religiously since launching my Think Digital First website and all of the corresponding online courses. There is also a new type of payment which has recently hit the market, which I will talk about in more detail.

PayPal

PayPal is used by more than 190 million people worldwide, and is by far the most successful and used payment gateway online. PayPal is available in 100 currencies, meaning that regardless of where your customers are from, they will have a seamless payment experience.

If PayPal was a bank, it would rank in the top 25 banks in the word...That's how influential and financially stable it is.

There are two main things I consider when choosing a payment gateway, and they are TRUST and SECURITY. Knowing that PayPal successfully deals with 9.3 million payments every day without fail makes me trust the brand, and therefore my audience will trust me for choosing that payment gateway.

As of 2017, the new ways to make payments are through Apple Pay or contactless payments. PayPal is now advertising a portable payment device which allows you to take contactless payments, saving you time when taking payments on the go.

Apple Pay

A new way of shopping has been introduced by Apple, and this is called Apple Pay. You can make secure purchases in shops, apps and now on the web, all from one simple app that lives on your smartphone.

If you are a physical shop, take a look at Apple Pay as a way of taking payments because more and more shoppers are now leaving the house without their wallet/purse; especially in London as the London Underground now accepts Apple Pay as a form of payment, along with the likes of Boots, Costa, M&S, Waitrose and New Look.

In my opinion, PayPal and Apple Pay are the two most important payment options to have as a business.

Stripe

Stripe handles billions of dollars every year, and is a forward-thinking company that helps small businesses take and manage payments online. If you're looking for a flexible tool for your online business that integrates seamlessly, and takes payments in an efficient way, take a look at Stripe.

SEARCH ENGINE OPTIMISATION

Now that you have the analytical tools (as mentioned above) how are you going to take the data from the analytics, and use this to create the perfect SEO/Metadata for your website?

These four tools will help you manage your specific keywords, and give you all of the information you need to better rank your business on Google.

Google Adwords Keyword Planner

Google Adwords Keyword Planner is a great free tool where you can build search campaigns. You can also look at searches based on keywords, and ad group ideas. You will be given statistics around your chosen keywords, and find out how competitive keywords are before actually spending any of your hard earned money.

Mangools

Mangools is a company developing SEO tools you will love. KWFinder is a well-known player among the top keyword research and analysis tools used by companies, bloggers, SEO and marketing agencies from all over the world. SERPChecker is a deep Google SERP analysis tool with 49+ SEO metrics to identify strengths and weaknesses of your competitors. They have been featured on PCMag, Hubspot, Backlinko and many other industry-leading sites.

Moz

Moz builds tools that make inbound marketing easy, backed by industry-leading data and the largest community of SEOs on the planet. It gives you the tools to measure website rankings, social traffic, website and SEO errors, as well as opportunities, research and custom reporting.

SEMrush

SEMrush is a powerful and versatile competitive intelligence suite for online marketing, from SEO and PPC to Social Media and video advertising research. The options are endless, and you can sign up for a free trial, and get a free two-hour online skype session where one of their employees will take you through their extensive features.

Yoast

And finally, Yoast is a great Wordpress plugin that allows you to optimise every web page and blog post on your website. It will rate your SEO on a traffic light system (red, orange and green), and give you a breakdown of what you can do to improve the SEO on each page of your website. I have been using Yoast as a guide to see that my keywords are where they should be on a blog, as well as making sure that all other key SEO metrics are being utilised.

DATA

Measuring the success of your business online is the key to understanding whether something is working, or whether you need to change your strategy. Without knowing the key analytical tools to help you achieve this, you will not be able to improve your strategy so that you are connecting with your audience in the way they want to be connected with.

When it comes to analytics, I have one particular dashboard that can be added to your Google Analytics account completely free of charge from my website.

Social Media Dashboard

My Social Media Dashboard will help you find out where your Social Media traffic is coming from, and what network is the highest converter for you so that you know where to focus your energy.

Google Analytics

For me, Google Analytics has been the go-to data tool. You can measure your website traffic, and where it is coming from. You can also go deeper, and measure your advertising ROI (return on investment) as well as tracking your Social Media conversions and your visitor demographic.

Google Analytics is a great, free and extensive tool that every business owner should be using.

Google Webmasters (Search Console)

Google's Search Console will track your site's search performance. You will have access to the data, tools, diagnostics and data you need to maintain your website, and create a Google-friendly website that will give you the results you are looking for.

Grytics

Facebook, for me, has been an amazing source of engagement over the last year and that purely because of Facebook Groups. I have a private members group which I engage with on a daily basis, and to analyse the data within the group I use an amazing tool called Grytics.

SIX

YOUR STRATEGY
AND IMPLEMENTATION PLAN

CHAPTER 6

"YOU CAN'T
SELL ANYTHING
if
YOU CAN'T
TELL ANYTHING "

This chapter, for me, is about bringing everything together to convert visitors into prospects and prospects into happy customers who become 24/7 brand advocates.

Having sold 1000's of copies of the first edition of this book, I decided to reach out to the readers and gather feedback, to really help me design a strategy based on where you are in your business right now, and how social media and digital marketing can truly work for you.

So based on the feedback I received, I've decided to break this chapter into three sections

1. The Preparation: Go-to-market strategy
2. Getting Started: Building trust with your audience
3. Business Growth: Generating leads and getting sales

Before we get started, let's remind ourselves of what we've learnt.

I've helped you to understand you and your customer and you've now had a mind-set shift.

I have also given you tools and tips to understand what it means to grow a business from managing your time and energy to designing a business.

You have been given the very latest technology to help your business go through a fast growth phase in the next 12 months by focusing on sales and marketing to prepare your business for success.

Now let the fun begin by taking all of your learnings and putting them into action, so you can help more customers solve their pain with your product or service.

THE PREPARATION PHASE

To make sure you and your team are prepared for every eventuality, you need a strategy and an actionable plan.

Do your homework on a prospective customer. There is no point picking up the phone to make a sales call without knowing how to fully express the benefits of your product in the right way, so that your customer responds positively. It's important that you know your pricing structure, based on selling different quantities, so you are not caught off guard when your customer requests this.

To help you, here is a simple four-step process and diagram. Using this will make sure you always know the steps you are taking are in the right direction, at the right time.

1. Go to Market Strategy
2. Marketing Plan
3. Sales Process
4. Customer Retention

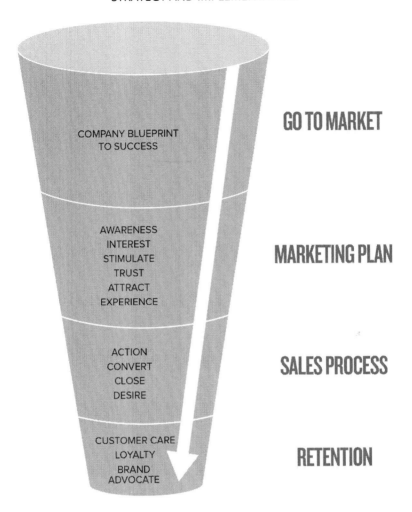

Download our 4-step process at thinkdigitalfirst.today.

Are you a business selling B2B and/or B2C, or a company which only works through organisations who sell direct to your specific target audience on your behalf?

Here is an example. Verisign (The company that owns .com, .org and many more) has a business model where they do not get on board any clients themselves. They only work with selective channel partners like GoDaddy or 123Reg who already have their target audience and license out domain names on their behalf.

At the other end of the spectrum is being the ONE company which everyone speaks to. For example; Gary Vaynerchuk. He is a front-facing brand and you connect to his business because of him, his brand and his market. His brand is solely built around his online profile.

On a small business scale, look at Levi Roots. He had an idea and passion to create a simple sauce and now he is worth more than £35 million. This is because of who he is and how his consumers have connected to his story.

You need to understand that you and your business are unique and the right process for you might not work for another, even if you're in the same business sector.

Unfortunately, it is common to see the wrong business models within organisations. Hopefully, if this is you, you will benefit from creating a business that achieves fast growth through being personal and relevant to your prospects.

Your company's situation is different from your competitors' and, as customers (taking our business hats off for a moment), we have evolved the www into this amazing new social web. It gives you a voice to openly talk about your positive experiences, making brands listen and changing the way they do business.

Go To Market Strategy

This is your company's blueprint, from which your overall sales and marketing plan evolves. Your business will share the value of its product or service by connecting with your laser targeted customers.

When deciding on your Go to Market Strategy, you need to include your entrepreneur leadership style and the type of culture you want to build. Look at the local, national and international environment of your industry/sector and the current capabilities of you and your team. Decide what's missing to fill the gap, and the various types of revenue streams which can flow into your business for growth. All of these form your blueprint and will ultimately mould the way you communicate your message to your target customer, and of course; tell your story.

Your Go to Market Checklist will include the following.

- ✔ Solving a need in the market which offers fast growth
- ✔ Understanding your opportunity in the market
- ✔ Knowing who your laser focused target market is for initial launch
- ✔ Identifying the influencers in your industry to be brand advocates
- ✔ Understanding the pain point which will help you know what the business problem is, and develop a unique selling proposition to solve it
- ✔ Discovering how you can be different from your competitors
- ✔ Preparing a product roadmap from idea to delivery
- ✔ Tracking and measuring your results
- ✔ Developing a sales and marketing plan integrated with a customer retention strategy
- ✔ Training your team in every aspect of the business process
- ✔ Identifying channel partners based on your target audience
- ✔ Completing your USP

When sharing the same USP with two different target customers (you might have a business that sells B2B and B2C) you must offer a different value proposition to help them understand what pain your problem solves and how it can help them.

Next, you need to design an actionable plan in the form of a document which lists what steps must be taken and by whom to achieve a specific goal.

Marketing

We've covered this in previous chapters, but marketing is in essence, identifying, anticipating and meeting the requirements of what your consumers want, to make a profit in your business. Putting the customers' wants and needs first will be identified through your market research.

Because your competitors might have the same target market as you, it doesn't mean they are ultimately solving their customers pain. You must be carrying out research to find out what your target market really wants from your specific business.

Ask your customers about your product or service. What improvements would they like to see? Once you know this, you can develop a range of products or services, suitable for your specific customer and they will love this.

So when it comes to marketing your brand, it's no longer as simple as the old AIDA sales process, which you have been using since 1904:

- building **Awareness**;
- gaining the **Interest**;
- sharing the **Desire**;
- getting the user to take **Action**.

These days you want more from your customers. You want loyalty, and you want them to talk about your brand and to become brand advocates. At each stage of your Go to Market Strategy you want them to buy from you. Whether this is an impulse buy in real-time, or a well thought through process that's taken months of research...it still matters.

New world business model: RENSA

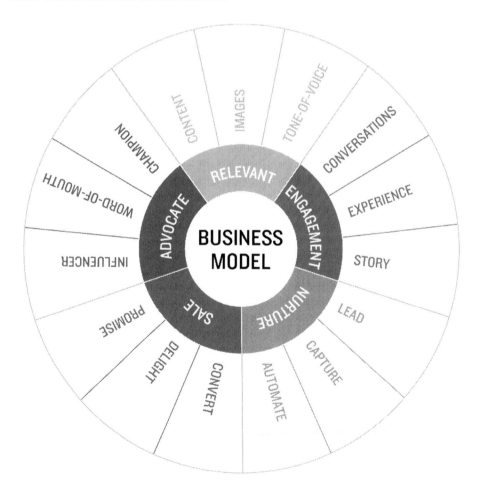

Download the RENSA Business Model at thinkdigitalfirst.today.

Relevant

By taking your content, and sharing this with images, you are building your tone of voice. This should be talking to your customers in the way they want to be talked to.

Engagement

Tell your story, give the customer an experience they fall in love with and have a real one-to-one conversation to build trust.

Nurture

Always be looking to deepen the relationship by taking the prospect out of social media using lead magnets and automating the start of the process as much as possible.

Sale

You have a promise you want to deliver to you customers once you have converted and delighted them.

Advocate

Once you have a customer, why not turn that customer into a raving fan and a brand advocate who talks to their community all about you?

Sales

Selling, on the other hand, is about persuading customers to buy your products/ services by helping them believe it is what they are looking for. This will take place once the marketing has influenced a customer's buying habit.

After you have completed your customer focused marketing, you introduce your product or service to your potential customer, by highlighting the features but selling through the benefits.

This might include the following;

- advertising and promotion;
- direct selling; and
- supporting literature.

Once you've effectively shared the benefits of your product and service to your potential customer through marketing your brand, you can engage with them through your sales process to the point of purchase. Marketing and sales go hand in hand because of this simple, but critical-to-get-right process.

Product driven business, for example, building a product led brand.

The fashion industry is known for having two seasons; spring/summer, autumn/ winter. Having worked in the retail industry for 25 years, I always come across the same problem. For a brand to get into the marketplace it must first invest in stock (unless you are a 100% drop shipping retailer). This stock potentially has a short life cycle because of the two seasons. Whilst you can discount your stock, it has an effect on your P/L (profit and loss) at the end of the year. The first route to market is having a business model which allows you to get forward orders on your stock at a wholesale price before the stock even arrives in your warehouse. You need an online store allowing you to sell at the RRP (recommended retail price) which offers you, the business owner, a massive margin from cost to sale price.

Your other route to market is selling direct to the customer through your website and potentially, pop-up shops and market stalls in specific locations. By selling direct to the customer, the value you bring is focused on your brand, the quality of the product, the personal service you offer and the fact that they are part of a community of customers who love your brand. The consumer wants to feel good about buying your product. They have no interest in making money from your product, not like your other route to market; your business owner.

These two routes to market have a different type of target customer and therefore the value that you give to those target customers has to be different. What do I mean by this? You're a brand who wants to sell into a high street store. The high street store has enough stock to last a season and it will buy various sizes and colours from your range, potentially spending ££££s with you at a wholesale price. This guarantees volume but does not guarantee a high margin. To achieve this, you might have to go to trade shows, travel and work with a distributor/agent to sell your products on your behalf and you may have to supply points of sale to help promote your brand in-store. More importantly, you are selling your product to the owner of the shop who knows their customer and knows they can make money from your brand. The value you bring to this target customer is the fact that you make them money.

Service Driven Business

This is where I've seen a massive shift in the market over the last three years, and those who have adopted the concept of digital marketing will really reap the rewards now, and in the future.

There are many service driven companies which sell direct to customers and sell direct to businesses. If you are a service driven business, you need to think about acquiring your customers through more than one sales avenue.

For example: if you are a consultancy firm specialising in sales, you need to think about more than one way of acquiring a customer to maximise the value you bring to a business, ultimately acquiring more customers and building your business. The more traditional way of acquiring a customer is going and sharing the value of your business with them. That person needs to see the value of what you can do for them and hire you to deliver that specific piece of work. Again, that individual is looking for a personal service, potentially looking to have their hand held throughout the process and for knowledge sharing, to ultimately help them upskill and develop their own strengths.

The other Go to Market Strategy for a service driven business is to find organisations which I call Channel Partners, who already have a database of your target customers. You work with that organisation to share the benefit of your services to their customers.

The value proposition to the Channel Partner is that they are on a commission for every one of their target customers who buy into your business. Also, they know that if your business delivers for their target customer, their customers will always remember them for making the introduction.

Ultimately, you must always be thinking about a minimum of three ways to bring different revenues into your business. This determines your business model and how you market your business online.

Below I have listed three ways I bring revenue into my business, I would like you to think and write down three ways you can bring revenue into yours.

1. Online Training
2. Professional Speaking
3. Coaching

I do have more than three but these are the ones that generate 80% of my revenue.

IDENTIFY 3 APPROPRIATE REVENUE STREAMS FOR YOUR BUSINESS
Identify the revenue streams and give the pros and cons of each.

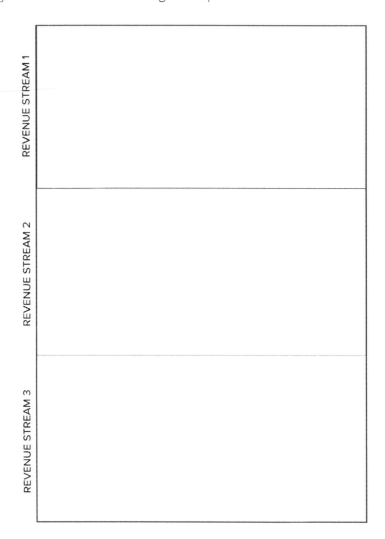

Always Think #Digital First. To get the most from your strategy, you must be laser focused on knowing your target customer (as mentioned in Chapter 2). Knowing their age, sex, income level, habits, interests, who they are and where they hang out, will help you understand their buying patterns.

Your timing is crucial in making sure the content you provide is personal, current, adds value and contributes to the buyer's purchasing journey.

Your 90-day Go to Market Strategy might look like this;

	30 DAYS	60 DAYS	90 DAYS
PEOPLE	What do we want to achieve?	Connect with decision makers on social networks	Send quotes & contract
PEOPLE	Who is going to implement	Build relationships	Implement retention strategy
PEOPLE	Branding yourself	Strategic hire	Expand the team
PROCESS	Key performance indicators	Implement & analyse	Take action
PROCESS	Budget	Extra costs?	What's the cost per lead?
PROCESS	Learn the technology	Other alternatives	Monitor and refine
TECHNOLOGY	Website	Work the issue	Get extra IT support
TECHNOLOGY	Content plan	Set IT goals	Measure & follow up
TECHNOLOGY	Tools to automate the message	Realign and stop what's not working	Stop and start the loop again

Download our 90 Day Go-to-market Strategy at thinkdigitalfirst.today.

1–30 days: Research and set goals
30–60 days: Develop the plan and start the execution
60–90 days: Follow up and analyse

By having a 90-day Go to Market Strategy, with a focus on Sales and Marketing, you will be able to keep the business moving forward, while holding each team member personally accountable for each of the actions needed.

You role is to constantly be working ON the business and not IN the business, meaning you are not involved in the day-to-day operations of the business. As the business owner, you need to know how you can take your business to the next level by implementing systems and procedures which enable it to run smoothly and have the strategy that's always growing brand awareness and increasing sales. This can only be done by taking a helicopter view of your business, competitors and industry; as things are always evolving, especially with the fast pace of technology, which is changing the way we work.

Marketing Plan
While it's important to know what's happening during the year in your business, for me, 90 days has always been the perfect time to prepare, implement and measure, to a real effect. Measuring one year after a campaign has finished will not have any effect on where your business is right NOW.

Your 90-day Marketing Plan will explain what your marketing strategy is and how it will be executed to generate increased brand awareness and drive targeted traffic into your sales process. When developing your Marketing Plan, you will need to ask yourself the following questions;

- How will you share your product/service?
- How will you entice potential customers to buy your product/service?
- How will you develop customer loyalty to develop repeat business and referrals?

Your marketing plan is created for your specific target audience which you have already identified. Keep reading to find out what you can include in your 90-day Marketing Plan.

90-Day Plan

The visual below is an example of a 90-day Marketing Plan, including when your business is going to market to your specific target audience. This template has a variety of offline and online marketing actions associated to a specific month. These actions and the month they happen will differ according to your business and the things you need to take into consideration before putting this plan together.

To help you, I've listed things you might want to think about.

- What time of year is your product mentioned online?
- When does your industry have a trade show?
- When are you launching a new product/service?
- Press Releases
- Industry Awards
- Channel Partner events
- Seasons; autumn/winter or spring/summer
- Competitions
- Networking events

MARKETING ACTION PLAN

TARGET

ACTIVITY	ACTION	Jun-18	Jul-18	Aug-18
Blog Ideas: clothes, country, events, local	West Essex Fashion Fair			
	Launch of New Top			
	Swimwear launch			
	*New Brand			
	Tour de France			
	Sale			
	Competition			
Newsletters	New in (Brands)			
	Launch of New Top			
	Swimwear	░	░	
	Sale	░	░	
	Competition			
Competitions	It's all about ME			
	Swimwear Giveaway	░		
	New Mums to be			
	Leather Jackets			░
Sale	Summer Stock		░	
	Winter Stock			
SEO	Whats New	■	■	■
	Dresses			
	Knitwear			
	Tops			
	Jackets			
	Trousers			
	Accessories			
	Brands	■		
Clothes Parties	Boutique X	■	■	
	Arbonne			
	Jamie at Home			
	Avon			

The download is colour-coded to help you stay focused on that specific action required in a particular month.

GETTING STARTED WITH THE BASICS: BUILDING TRUST PHASE

Now we're going to help you share relevant content to your visitors and prospects through a simple and easy-to-follow weekly plan in just 60 minutes for seven days' worth of content.

This plan is different from what I wrote in the first edition because of how social networks have evolved, where your potential target customers hang out, and the way they like to be communicated with.

Now you've decided what actions you're going to take during the next 90 days, let's define what content you're going to share, using various tools and marketing platforms, with my seven day content media marketing plan.

As mentioned in Chapter 4, Content Marketing is the sharing of media and published content to reach more customers as part of the customer acquisition journey, and increase your sales. This includes everything from products, news, blogs, PR, videos, white papers, e-books, Infographics, case studies and images, all of which can be shared across multiple channels with keywords in every message you share. This will come from the original SEO research document you prepared about the business in Chapter 4.

7-Day Social Media And Content Marketing Plan

By following this step-by-step process, which takes 60 minutes to complete, you will be able to manage all your social media in just 20 minutes a day and share all of your valuable content to your target audience knowing that every image, tweet, blog and post has been designed to talk to your customer about your business.

From a best practice perspective, I recommend the following 3:2:1 Rule:

- 3 tweets a day
- 2 posts a day Instagram and Pinterest
- 1 post a day on Facebook and Google+
- 1 blog a week

For me, one tweet at two three-hour intervals from 7am-7pm works, however once you've spent time analysing your online audience, the results could give you the following for the best times to publish content:

➡ 8am
➡ 1pm
➡ 6.30pm

With Twitter, every tweet must be from 100-120 characters including the shortened URL, based on the following strategy;

First tweet of the day could be a fun fact about your product/service

Second tweet about your blog of the week or industry article

Third tweet is company news (new product/service coming soon/preview, an event, competition, press release, product on sale, new store, new product, trivia, behind the scenes, what's happening with the team, team challenges, testimonials, events, pictures of staff, old blog (if run out of contents)

Over the seven days of the week you might want to mix things up:

Friday: Focus on blog of the week, competition announcement (when it happens, takes precedence)
Saturday: About your product/service
Sunday: Company information
Monday: Staff at work, profile, trips etc
Tuesday: Global industry news
Wednesday: Another product/service or new product/service coming soon (carrot dangling)
Thursday: Focus on a customer, thanking them for their referral or recommendation.

As you've read in Chapter 4, over the past three years these three forms of content marketing have exploded, and with this explosion have come complexities to promoting your brand online, so let's break this down bit by bit.

Images: There are four different ways to use images to help promote your business through organic, paid and influencers.

Here, we break down where your brand assets live online, and how they are used.

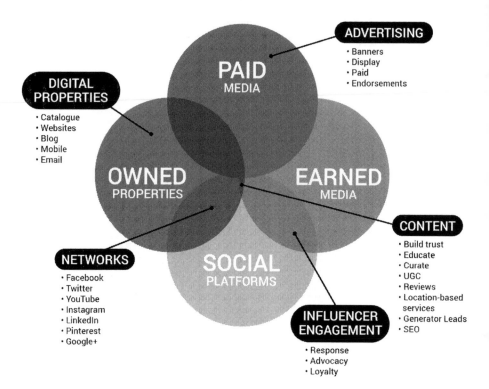

GIF's

An animated GIF (Graphics Interchange Format) file is a graphic image on a Web page that moves. For example; a moving icon or a display banner with a moonwalking hip hop dancer or numbers that magically get smaller and bigger.

Video

Is now one of the best ways to tell a story around your brand. I have found this to be one of the most popular ways to get a message across quickly and easily and with the use of a smartphone, we can all become movie makers.

Hashtags

If there is one thing that truly confuses people when they first get started with social media, it's hashtags. I'm going to try and simplify this for you and give a best practice for each social network.

A hashtag is a label for content. It helps others who are interested in a certain topic quickly find content on that same topic.

With Pinterest I recommended anything from 5-10 hashtags on every post and on all the other social networks I recommend no more than two.

For use across all of your social networks;

Location: #London | #UK | #Shoreditch
Brand: #Google | #Asos #Hootsuite
Product/Service: #Swimwear #CRM #Email
Target Customer: #Entrepreneur #Female #Foodie

Now you know what type of content you're going to use, the focused subject to talk about and at what time across which network, it's time to gather the information in a simple and easy to use document.

Here is an example, on the next page. It's time for you to fill in day one of your seven day plan and then download the full seven day template.

1 DAY SOCIAL MEDIA PLAN

DAY 1	HR 1 - 0900 UK	HR 2 - 1100 UK	HR 3 - 1300 UK	HR 4 - 1500 UK	HR 5 - 1700 UK
TWITTER + LINKEDIN	WK Blog Thank you @e_nation for including me as a Top 10 Business Advisor http://ow.ly/IgNir #BusinessGrowth	Visual Quote Social Media Picture Quote of the Day - http://ow.ly/BsRjP #SocialMedia #Marketing	Education tweet from Feedly Did you know @warrenknight will be talking at @... on the (date) about #Socialmedia #digital (link to seminar page)	WK Blog #Hootsuite Review: 7 Features You Need to Use http://ow.ly/ #Technology	Education tweet from Feedly How To Create Headlines That Get Clicks #Infographic - http://ow.ly/IgQKa
FACEBOOK		Take the latest WK blog on www.warren-knight.com and use above hashtags when suitable (no more than 2)			
PINTEREST + INSTAGRAM Important # Same format as Twitter		Take WK blog and add to "Blogs" board with picture			
G+ Important # Same format as Facebook		Post as you would on Facebook			

Download the 7-day Social Media Plan at thinkdigitalfirst.today.

Once you've filled in seven days of content, which will take only one hour, use a tool mentioned in Chapter 5 to schedule to Twitter, Facebook, LinkedIn and Google+.

Schedule using Schedugram for Instagram, Viralwoot for Pinterest (as mentioned in Chapter 5).

Here's my 20-minute a day plan, now you've automated your content across multiple social networks.

9 minutes a day:
At 9am, 1pm and 7pm, spend three minutes thanking people for liking, commenting and sharing your updates.

5 minutes:
Spend five minutes retweeting, and engaging with prospects, clients or industry influencer's posts.

5 minutes:
Follow five new prospects and include them in on a social media post.

1 minute:
Check your analytics to make sure what you're doing is working

BUSINESS GROWTH: GENERATING LEADS AND GETTING SALES

Now I'm going to let you into some of the secrets I use in the sales and marketing process that has enabled me to grow one of my companies to £1 million in less than two years. Since then, I have built multiple six-figure businesses in less than 12 months and have won various awards and accolades like being a Top 100 Global Influencer.

Let's stay positive, You're growing your followers, getting engagement and building your brand awareness. It's now time to take all of your hard work and turn those followers into prospects in a simple three-step process by implementing the strategy to get new customers.

Step One
Adding a CTA (call to action) at the end of your updates will give the visitor the opportunity to come over to your website to view a specific piece of content like a blog, white-paper, case-study, discount code, BOGOF etc. On this page you will ask the visitor to get a copy of the specific give-away, which this is better known as a 'lead magnet'. In other words, something you give away for free to attract a lead (prospect).

Step Two
Once you've captured their name and email address we can deepen the relationship by adding more value to them with a series of emails that include more images, videos, added value content, basically educating the prospect on how you can help them. This is better known as 'Marketing Automation'.

Below is a simple automation process for you to follow:

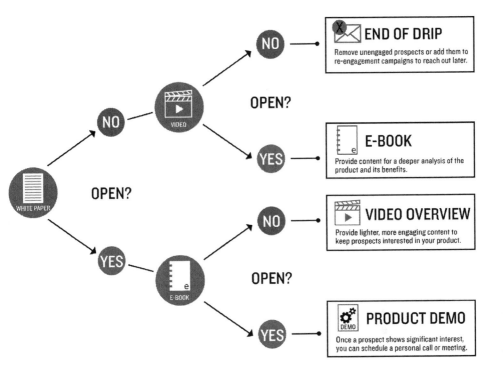

Step Three

This is the final step in the process, but the one most companies miss – ultimately losing the prospect and wasting all their hard work.

Let's recap the process so far.

You've now found a visitor inside social media, they've clicked on a link taking them to your website, and they've downloaded a 'lead magnet' and are now a part of your marketing automation process.

Every piece of technology has some form of small data for you to look at, and one of the great features inside tools like Mailchimp and Active Campaign is that you can actually see who has clicked on the links inside the specific marketing automation process. This will give you the most engaged people in the process and tells you they are very interested in what you're selling, giving you a 'warm prospect' to...

"PICK
—— up the ——
PHONE,,

When was the last time you picked up the phone, had a conversation with a prospect and converted them into a customer?

Great places to find the prospect whose email you captured with your lead magnet are their website and LinkedIn profile, where people will add their website, email address and landline and mobile.

To simplify the process even more, here are some quick tips to help you devise your sales process to turn that prospect into a customer.

Set simple and achievable goals on a daily basis.

- Make three warm calls
- Send five emails to introduce yourself and the business
- Arrange two face to face meetings
- Create no less than two proposals
- Make no less than two presentations
- Run one webinar (might only be monthly)
- Speak at a networking event (start with one a month)

You can download my simple 10-day spreadsheet to help you track and analyse the results on www.thinkdigitalfirst.today. Don't forget to always put the data into your CRM (as mentioned in Chapter 5).

	Monday	Tuesday	Wednesday	Thursday	Friday
Touch Base Calls to potential customers					
Total per day	11	4	3	9	5
Client Calls - Minimum 2 per day					
Call 1	Call John S	Call James W	Call Daryl W	Call Patrice H	
Call 2	Call Sarah H	Call Chris G		Call Karl P	
		Call Jane M			
Meetings - Minimum 1 per day					
Meeting 1	Meeting with ASOS		Meeting with GA	Breakfast meeting	Meeting Ryan
Meeting 2			Meeting with Innovate Centre	Meeting with Post Office	Meeting Oak
Meeting 3					Meeting Relish
Events		Launch party			
Seminars	See Warren Speak				Google campus
Targets for meetings over next 5 days	2	2	2	2	2
Actual (over next 5 days)	3	1	1	2	3
Needed / Surplus	1	-1	-1	0	1

If making calls is something that you don't enjoy doing, here is a step-by-step structure to help you stay in control of the conversation and make sure you're helping the caller at each stage of the process and always getting the results THEY want:

Stage 1:
Introduce yourself
Build rapport

Stage 2 - Pre-Frame:
30 mins for this call
Find out what you can about THEM
Answer their questions to get the results YOU want
At the end of the call, how you are going to move forward together?

Stage 3:
Tell me about YOU
Tell me about your business What is your main driver for success? Is it your family? Money? Freedom? Want to succeed? And, what's your vision for the business?

Stage 4 - What They Want:
Go back to the difficulty, and ask for more feedback using the below as guidelines.
- Why is that?
- Explain more
- Can you elaborate on that for me please?
- What do you mean?

- Why is that important? Rate on a scale of 1-10
- What are the barriers?
- Go into more depth (about keywords mentioned)
- How important is that to you, on a scale of 1-10 - so I can get the idea
- Am I right in saying "You want more traffic from Facebook (example)" explain the process based on how you see it.
- Small amount first - make them see the problem
- What concerns you the most: Time? Money? Or, certainty? Play it back again: Is it the time you don't have to spend on this? Is it to shorten the time to get to where you want to be? You are missing out on money, by not taking action now.

Stage 5:
In a perfect world, what would you want to happen, and how much would you pay for that?

Stage: Pre-Close:
- How do you feel things are going?
- Do you think we can work together?
- Do you have any other reservations?
- Did I understand YOU?

This is where you need to understand each other. At the end of the call, what's the next step?

Moving Forward
At the end of your call, you should schedule a meeting to discuss your proposition further. This can either be at your office, or a mutual location agreed by you and the potential customer. You should have your objectives and a plan of what you want to talk about in that meeting. You need to be as engaging as possible, otherwise your sales process will stop here. Achieving customer buy-in for your brand is essentially asking them to buy into you as well. You are representing your business and your passion needs to shine through. There is only one of you, and that alone makes you unique. Make sure your business shares the same uniqueness.

GROWTH HACKING
Growth hacking is another term that's evolved in the last three years, and refers to a set of both conventional and unconventional marketing experiments that lead to business growth .

Growth hackers are marketers that specifically focus on building and engaging the user base of a business.

Here are some of my favourites that you can implement in your business, some easier than others.

Facebook > Chatbots

Look into using Chatbots to automate your engagement and turn visitors into prospects. Chatbots is a computer program designed to simulate conversation with human users, especially over the Internet, and Facebook is leading the way with millions of conversations happening all over the world

Twitter > Images

When adding an image to your post, you can TAG 10 prospects into the image. Once published, Twitter informs the user that they have been mentioned and shows them your post.

Pinterest > Emails To Connect With Your Prospects

1. Set up an event on Eventbrite or run a Google Hangout on Google+
2. Promote it on all social networks
3. Upload an image into Pinterest in a suitable board
4. Edit the pin and add all the @names you are following and click 'Save'. Pinterest will email all the people saying they have been mentioned
5. Go back in and remove the @... @...
6. Wait for people to sign up

Remember: You must follow the people you want Pinterest to email. If you don't follow, then no @.... so you won't be able to email to that person.

Google > 1st Page Of Google

This is the only reason why I use Google+.

When I do a status update of an article or lead magnet that's on my website, Google (the search engine) knows it's come from my website. If you do this, when someone goes to Google and does a search, if your post inside Google+ matches the search term of the visitor, Google will bring your update from your Google+ account and place it on the 1st page of Google

To finish this chapter, I'd like to give you the three most successful tactics I use over and over again to win new business.

GOING TO NETWORKING EVENTS

Acquiring a new customer using technology and old school ways is powerful. Here are some of the tactics I use when going to an event when I know a potential prospect will be there;

- Connect with them on all social networks
- Say "hi" in LinkedIn before the event
- Meet and build rapport, get business card
- Send email to say hi and offer a lead magnet
- They download it and are added to a marketing automation
- Track open rate
- Connect inside of LinkedIn InMail to arrange a call
- Call and go through my call structure as covered earlier on in this chapter
- Arrange a meeting
- Follow up and close

WORKING WITH NEW CHANNEL PARTNERS

This has been one of the best tactics I've implemented to make sure I always have a pipeline of new customers.

1. Get your personal, admin, or virtual assistant to collate a list of companies which have your target audience and include the decision maker's name, email, telephone number, company website and all social media accounts.

2. Put the name and email address into an email-marketing tool like MailChimp and send a laser targeted email to the list.

3. Three days later, look at the analytics and see who has opened the email, it will tell you who and how many times.

4. Now you know who is interested in what you have to say, go and follow them across their social media platforms and like, retweet and share some information, so your brand is visible to them.

5. Pick up the phone and take them through your sales structure that I explained earlier in this chapter.

This gives you the opportunity to contact the 'low hanging fruit' of companies which four days ago might have never heard of you. Now they've received an email, a re-tweet, and a phone call, but you've only focused on the companies which have shown an interest and this data came from the open rate in MailChimp, saving you time and making sure you are getting a good ROI on your time.

You'll notice a common theme here. After an action is taken, I look at the data and then take a deeper action, helping me win new business.

GETTING REFERRALS

Within 30 days of delivering my product, service or solution, I will ask each of my new customers for at least three names and phone numbers of someone they know who may have a use for my products, services and solutions.

I also ask for a recommendation on LinkedIn and confirm if it's OK to publish it on my website. This will ultimately help me build social proof with future visitors and prospects.

SEVEN

IMPROVING YOUR CUSTOMER LOYALTY

CHAPTER 7

You have now gone through this book, and I hope that at this point you have learnt a lot, and taken all the steps to grow your business through online marketing.

Throughout this chapter, I'm going to be talking about the best ways to increase customer retention, and why I feel that building your personal brand is an important part of building a successful business.

You've now optimised your content so it's search-friendly, adds real value and explains how you help your customers by sharing content on a daily, weekly and monthly basis. By continuously sharing this content, you are automatically building loyalty with your customers and you are continuously focusing on your brand awareness and gaining market share.

Over the last three years my personal focus has been on building my personal brand. When I wrote the final chapter of this book for the first edition, I focused on the importance of technology and using this to achieve your customer retention outcome. Now, rewriting this book and especially this chapter, I reached out to my peers and customers within the industry and got feedback from them on the one thing that made them keep on wanting to work with me. Unanimously, they said it's because of how I've grown my personal brand online, and how I utilise customer loyalty and brand advocates who will happily go and talk about my business to their community.

Customer loyalty should be at the forefront of your customer retention strategy. Your business will now be working with your customers daily, through sharing added-value content which has been designed to help your company get noticed across the new social web.

"POTENTIAL ONLINE CUSTOMERS
— are touched by a brand —
8 TIMES BEFORE PURCHASING"

As previously mentioned, turning your visitors to turn into leads and paying customers, will, on average, require them to 'touch' your business eight times. Once they become a customer, they will want to share the added value content with their community, ultimately becoming a brand advocate and a loyal customer for your business.

"82% OF CONSUMERS
—have ended their relationship—
WITH A COMPANY DUE TO POOR CUSTOMER SERVICE"

As a business, you need to be constantly innovating and taking action to retain customers through loyalty. Before you can understand the strategies for this, you should know that 82% of customers have left a company because of a bad customer service experience. The big question is: What are you doing to retain customers? When it comes to customer retention, consider the following:

SET EXPECTATIONS
From the get-go, make sure you set realistic expectations with your customers. I cannot stress the importance of this enough. It is better to under-promise and over-deliver than to set an expectation with your clients, knowing you will have a hard time delivering on that promise. This will allow you to eliminate uncertainty and help you to ensure your client's happiness on delivery of a product or service.

A customer is more likely to remember a negative experience and share this with their community. Say you over-deliver on a service or product a number of times with the same customer and under-deliver just once; this is what they will remember and will, ultimately, be their reason for terminating a contract or choosing a competitor to purchase products from.

BUILD RELATIONSHIPS THAT LEAD TO TRUST ONLINE AND OFFLINE
A great business is built on trust and loyalty, and these are two of the biggest reasons a consumer will purchase a product or service on more than one occasion. Trust is an essential part of building relationships, especially through shared values in a service driven environment.
When you are working with a Channel Partner, shared values mean showing your interest in your client and their business. Understand the role you play

in helping their business grow, while at the same time building a working relationship through loyalty.

I work with a number of Channel Partners in different sectors, and part of our partnership is for me to build trust within their community not only by speaking at their events, but also by running webinars, writing content and engaging with their following through Social Media.

Your potential customers need help now more than ever and just posting content and hoping to develop a relationship will not work. You need to find out what they want from you, and how you can deliver it.

ANTICIPATE CUSTOMER SERVICE ISSUES

Be proactive and deal with issues around customer service before they even arise. Remember not to wait for something to happen. Put a plan into action to eliminate any problems, before they become a roadblock to retaining a customer. Zopim, a live chat tool, which I spoke about in Chapter 5, is a great way to catch a potential customer when they most need help, and solve any issues before that customer decides to look elsewhere.

For example, a major airline will text a customer to advise them of flight delays, avoiding issues around them not being aware of it. As an entrepreneur, you need to put yourself in your customers' shoes. Take a proactive approach to what could become a negative experience.

AUTOMATION

Automation is an online form of a repeatable process which, when done right, will help you save time, develop relationships and increase loyalty.

You should know from Chapter 3 which tasks are going to be time-consuming for you and from Chapter 5 which tools to use to help you with this. Customer retention using online automated messages is a way you can leverage your business, without having to take constant action to add value and retain loyal customers.

To give you an example, I have various side-products in the form of complementary guides and resources that are free to download from my ThinkDigitalFirst.com website. For someone to download this free piece of content, they have to give me their name and email address. This is me taking a visitor on my website, and turning them into a prospect.

To take this prospect, and turn them into a customer, there is a huge gap where I need to build trust and authority with this prospect. To bridge this gap, I use ActiveCampaign to set up a series of emails that get sent out automatically to a segmented group of my email database. I also use this same strategy when someone has signed up to a webinar of mine. They receive a selection of emails over 14 days where I give, give and give. Then, when I know that they can trust what I say, and have gotten to know 'me', I can then upsell my product which can turn into a sale.

We are becoming more and more time short, and because of this we must find a way to still engage and reach our audience, without it taking away from building a business. I always say Social Media will not fix a broken business and this couldn't be more true this year.

If you are going to automate your Social Media content, you must have a clear goal in mind for what you want to achieve. Collect your data, use your tools to analyse this and then automate your content on Social Media to achieve your outcome.

BUILD KPI'S (KEY PERFORMANCE INDICATORS)

Improving customer service will ultimately boost how many customers you retain. To help you achieve this, establish your SMART KPIs; Specific, Measurable, Achievable, Relevant and Time-based. This helps you understand what is damaging your customer retention and how you can improve it.

See BELOW, and having now gone through the book, and defined your KPIs, fill out your SMART goals.

S.M.A.R.T. GOALS
━━━ WORKSHEET ━━━

Specific

> What exactly do I want to do?

Measurable

> How will I track my progress?

Attainable

> Is this realistic for me? Do I have what I need to make it possible?

Relevant

> Why am I doing this? Does it matter to me?

Time-oriented

> When will I have this completed?

Download the S.M.A.R.T. Goals Template at thinkdigitalfirst.today.

Understand that everything you create as a business, and all of the content you share online, must have performance indicators so that you can understand what is working, and what is not. Knowing what works will help you build great customer retention, whilst also building your personal brand.

GO ABOVE AND BEYOND

Your customers expect you to go above and beyond, as they know what loyalty means to businesses. Take a mobile phone service provider for example. When you call them to upgrade your phone, you expect not to have your contract fee increased and not to pay a single penny for the device. This can be difficult, but as soon as you play the loyalty card, they will go above and beyond to make sure that you are getting the deal you deserve and that they get you for at least another 18 months as a returning customer.

> **"RESEARCH YOUR CUSTOMERS** *to see* **WHAT THEY WANT "**

FEEDBACK SURVEYS

Customer feedback surveys are one of the best ways to show your customers that you are listening to what they have to say and want to improve the service you offer them. This is invaluable for learning your customers' expectations. In Chapter 5 I shared a great survey tool which use.

After every online course I run, I will always ask my attendees for their feedback, and to give scores based on the content they received. Really use this information to better your products/services, and if you do find that one of your customers is unhappy with your business, find a way to work with them, and solve this issue.

SHOPPING CART ABANDONMENT

Have you ever followed one of your customer's journeys through Google Analytics and seen that they have got to the payment page and then suddenly left your website? You don't need to see it happen to know that it is definitely happening. The average shopping cart abandonment rate for e-Commerce is an astounding 65-75%, and is as much as 97% on mobile. This means that you are losing a large amount of business and, unfortunately, even the best shopping cart solutions can't find a guaranteed fix.

There are some steps you can take to ensure you are doing everything to reduce that 65% for your business.

1. Free shipping;
2. Simplify the checkout process;
3. One-click payment;
4. Get rid of hidden charges; and
5. Offer real time support.

GOOGLE IS YOUR BEST FRIEND

Google is a business's best friend. I found this out when they mentioned me in a Google+ post, on their official Google Analytics page to more than 3.3 million followers. What better brand advocate can you get? This wouldn't have happened if I wasn't blogging on a regular basis about relevant and interesting content. Blogging is a part of your customer retention and marketing strategy, which I spoke about in Chapter 4.

Let's move on to a very important part of understanding where your visitors are coming from, when they are leaving and how you can make it easier for them to use and stay on your website. I previously mentioned Google Analytics as a tool in Chapter 5. Here is a guide to helping you use it for your business.

1. Adding The Code
Once you have set up your account on Google Analytics, you will need to add the code they give you, into the back end of your website. This is so you can accurately track all activity.

2. Knowing What You Can Measure
After you have inputted the code, click on 'view report' on the screen, which will bring you to the main dashboard. There are various types of data you can measure which includes visitors, traffic sources, content, goals and eCommerce. What you track depends on what you want to achieve.

3. Setting Up Your Dashboard
There is a main dashboard where you will see an overview of your data. This is customisable. You can choose to see any of your reports from this area and also more detail around each report. Click 'view report'.

4. Adjusting The Time Range

Google Analytics will by default give you your results based on a one-month period. You can change this by adjusting the date range.

As well as all of the above, you can use Hootsuite to manage your social media analytics. Hootsuite allows you to combine real-time social actions taking place around your networks with an engagement solution, giving you access to data, which you can take immediate action on.

This tool allows you to;
- Track your brand growth;
- Visualise social demographics;
- Measure sentiment metrics;
- Identify social influencers;
- See what content resonates; and
- Create detailed social reports.

PERSONALISATION

When building a successful business you make every action you take around your customer personalisable. When sending a survey to your customers, get their date of birth so you can send a special discount/gift and written card on their birthday. It will be an unexpected, but very much appreciated, surprise.

With every order new client you acquire, if you're a product driven business, maybe go down the 'old-school' route of sending a personal, handwritten message so they know you appreciate their purchase.

From making a good first impression to tailored emails, personalisation and mobile customisation, you are making sure that your customers know what they want and that their needs come first.

56% of marketers believe that personalised content encourages a higher engagement rate and I can definitely agree with this statistic. When I write an article I share my stories, and the way I action a lot of my tips and tricks, as well as giving the reader an insight into who I am. Are you doing the same?

Personalisation is one of the most effective customer retention tips for businesses online as a way to really connect with their audience on a personal level and encourage repeat sales.

Having a customer retention strategy is key, because happy customers are what will ultimately drive your business forward. Customer retention will also give your brand exposure which in turn, will build your personal brand online.

Building a personal brand, and becoming an expert in your industry, is what will bring you success as a business owner marketing online.

Facebook has the success it has because of Mark Zuckerberg, and the same goes for Apple with Steve Jobs. I could name hundreds of entrepreneurs who sit in front of their business, and have achieved so much success by putting a name and face to their creation.

"EVERY STORY STARTS WITH AN IDEA
but it's the
CHARACTERS THAT MOVE THE IDEA FORWARD"

Trust should be at the forefront of connecting with your customers online. Trust and authority are what drives a business forward. I know you're probably reading this and thinking that you are HAPPY to sit behind your brand, and would rather allow your business to excel whilst you watch from the sidelines.

Becoming an expert in your industry is something you shouldn't be scared of. I remember when I was the CEO and co-founder of my eCommerce platform and how daunting it was thinking about being the person who was 'attached' to the business. Wherever I went, people would recognise my name as the person who co-founded this amazing company, which was exciting.

When I had to liquidate the company, I was also the person who had to take a step back and re-evaluate my professional life. I delivered the bad news to the investors, and also to myself, but without experiencing this, I wouldn't have understood the importance of building a personal brand, and becoming an expert.

My setbacks in 2013 are what got me to where I am today, and have given me the success I imagined was possible. I wanted to share that with you because I went through so many ups and downs, and becoming the expert I am today was one of the best decisions I have ever made.

It has taken me almost 10 years to build a strong personal brand online and I want to try and fast track you, so that can put yourself in front of your brand and feel proud about how you are being perceived online.

WHY DOES HAVING A PERSONAL BRAND MATTER?

You have a business, and you are marketing this business online. You are also attending tradeshows, events and meetups where you talk about your business to potential customers, or partners of yours.

They want to get to know YOU; the person behind the brand. Remember that people always buy from people, so putting yourself at the forefront of your business is crucial to its longevity and success.

Think about the contacts you have built in your industry, and the people you speak to and connect with on a day-to-day basis. To give your business the best possible chance, you must make sure that you are consciously building your personal brand and getting YOUR voice heard.

Here's how you can build your personal brand.

Use Stereotypes To Your Advantage

I'm sure you're reading this shaking your head but first, hear me out. When you want to give an accurate impression of your personal brand, you need to make this relatable, which is why it is OK to identify with a stereotype. The chances are, your audience are already thinking this way.

After identifying the stereotype, then identify the assumption that goes along with this. Whilst I wear nice clothes and drive a BMW, I am also extremely hardworking, and always have been since a very young age. Identifying this will allow you to get ahead of the stereotype and become a REAL person.

Be A Real Person

It is easy to label or stereotype someone, but when this happens you need to find a way to make sure you are truly being identified as a REAL human being. I'm Warren Knight rather than an average height male who is married with a baby. Yes, I am all of those things. But I don't let them define me, but rather, share them as experiences in my growth as a personal brand.

Manage Your Reputation

Part of building a strong personal brand is understanding where you need to make changes. There may be a slight gap between your brand and your reputation.

Ask yourself this question; what three words would YOU associate with yourself? Once you have your three words, ask someone you trust the same question. If they don't match up, think about why this is, and whether this is reflecting a gap between your brand and reputation.

After asking those closest to me, the three words that kept coming up were:
1. Driven
2. Passionate
3. Knowledgeable.

What are your three words?

1. _____

2. _____

3. _____

Make The Change
After you've found the difference between how you are perceived, and the reality of your personal brand, you might need to make some adjustments. Start with what is going to be the biggest change for your personal brand and work from there.

Be Approachable
80% of success is just showing up. Make yourself available and approachable. I run monthly webinars, as well as sharing with my audience where they can attend a seminar of mine. This alone is me showing up, and being approachable.

Say What You Mean, And Mean What You Say
Change people's perception of you by being honest and staying true to your word. Don't overcomplicate things. I know what works for my community as I have spent the last three years fine-tuning my written and visual content so that when someone comes across one of my articles, they know it's from me.

Over the last seven chapters I have taken you through the process of becoming an entrepreneur and building a business. I hope that you've found this book helpful, and that you will be able to grow your business through using all the tips, tools, strategies and templates I have shared with you.

Now turn over the page to read the summary, where I bring this book to a close and highlight the importance of getting online and taking the steps to growing your business.

Start today by creating your online brand identity and putting registering a memorable business domain name at the top of your to-do list.

SUMMARY

Writing the second version of this book has been a challenge, but one that has been amazing, and extremely rewarding. Before you reach the end of this book, I just want to summarise the best learnings from this book, so that you can continue to grow as an entrepreneur who wants to build their online identity, make a difference in the world and in doing so, make their business a thriving success.

As an entrepreneur and deciding what you want to do, the best tip I can give you is to focus your energy on being the most successful "you". Being a successful "you" means taking time out for yourself, focusing on what you love and overcoming the struggles you may face as an entrepreneur. Everything I have learnt as a business owner who wants a work lifestyle, and not a work-life balance has helped mould every single word I have written in this book.

Think about your business goals and where you want to take your business in the next 12 months. I knew that building an online training business from the ground up like I have would prove difficult. Having the structure in place by first choosing a memorable domain name not only built my online identity, but allowed me to understand my target audience, define my business, and appreciate the journey my audience go through from being a visitor to being a prospect and then a happy customer.

The way I was working three years ago is very different from today. My energy levels are at their optimum before the afternoon and that can be from 5am to 3pm, so when it comes to being creative, managing my team, speaking to new channel partners and focusing on building my online identity through two .com websites, this is my "prime time". The lesser important tasks such as admin and emails all come later in the afternoon and depending on your "prime time," manage your time in the way that works best for you.

If you're looking at all of the social networks mentioned in this book and realise that you don't have the time or knowledge to utilise them, employ an expert to help you achieve this. Use a freelancing platform like UpWork, because 96%[1] of customers are looking online for local products/services and if you are not utilising keywords so that you can be found online, you may miss out on vital sales for your business.

---

[1] Verisign data, June 2016

I have shared over 50 amazing tools that will help you research and listen to your audience, create content your audience will love and market your business through various Digital Marketing avenues. Business growth through building your online identity is key, especially when it comes to your website, and your domain name. Make your domain name as memorable as possible when choosing your .com, and always register more than one domain, just like I did when I registered thinkdigitalfirst.com and think-digital-first.com.

You can't sell anything, if you can't tell anything. Having sold 1,000's of copies of version one of this book, I decided to reach out to YOU, the readers, for feedback to really help me design a strategy based on where you are in your business right now and how social media and digital marketing can truly work for you as a business.

It's true that maintaining brand loyalty online can be one of your biggest problems as a business owner. A potential prospect will "touch" your business online six to eight times[2] before making a purchase, so brand consistency and trust online is key. Think about how you can build a consistent business through every step you take, including your approach to Social Media, as well as your website and the domain name you choose. And finally, don't let getting online intimidate you. This is a key part to achieving online success as a business. Take a look at all of the options available to you, and start small by registering a .com domain for your business.

Use this book as your workbook for success, and get online today. I would love to hear your feedback and thoughts on this book, so please reach out to me on Twitter @WarrenKnight, or visit www.thinkdigitalfirst.com for more great resources to help your business growth as a modern day entrepreneur.

Sponsored by Verisign.

---

[2] https://www.salesforce.com/blog/2015/04/takes-6-8-touches-generate-viable-sales-lead-heres-why-gp.html